LIVE
UNFROZEN

Superior Systems to Move
from Paralysis to Progress

Published by Nathan Ogden
Boise, ID
www.NathanOgden.com

For ordering information or special discounts for bulk purchases, please contact Nathan Ogden at 1.208.761.2770.

Book Design by Daniel Ruesch
www.danielruesch.net

Cover design by Barry Hansen

ISBN: 978-1530681983

Dedication

To my amazing wife Heather who has always shown endless love and support throughout this adventure together.

To my children Seniya, Kyler, Malani and Cortlyn for giving me desire and dreams I never knew I had.

And to all those who have ever thought it's too hard or you could never accomplish "that," or you're just not worth the effort — you are capable of greatness once you choose to attain it.

Acknowledgments

Growing up I always dreamed of marrying a beautiful, smart, talented woman, but I never thought it would actually happen. Heather is all of that and so much more. She has been the rock in my life that gives hope, strength, and direction. We are unstoppable together, no matter what we aspire to accomplish, fully admitting that she puts forth 70% of the effort most of the time. She is my motivation to seize each moment in life and the constant reminder that true love and devotion cannot be broken. Her desire to see me succeed is remarkably unselfish and driven. I love and adore her more than words allow.

A gigantic thank you to my remarkable children Seniya (16), Kyler (15), Malani (11), and Cortlyn (9). Being their father pushes me to get up on those days that I struggle, so I can be a part of their lives and discover even greater joy through their experiences and success. Their love and sacrifices on my behalf will never be forgotten.

Over the last 14 years I have learned invaluable lessons, molding me into the person I have become today. It would be ungrateful of me to think these core values were not instilled in me long before my ski accident. Being the son of Marshall and Jolene Ogden, I was taught the importance of faith in God, hard work and a "never-give-up" attitude. I married into a family led by Ron and Cheryl Fuller who shared a strong belief in these same essential principles, and for that I will always be thankful. You four have never doubted me.

My brothers and sisters on both sides of the family, along with their spouses, have given me the traction I needed when slipping backwards. They have cooked meals, been my handymen around the house, thrown me on four wheelers for a fun ride, traveled long distances to visit, and taken care of my family when I couldn't.

To all our friends who have helped in any way, I say thank you. You've called, visited, served and said innumerable prayers on our behalf. Our pantry was filled time and again because of your kindness, but more importantly you lifted our spirits. Knowing you were there gave me a safety net I could rely on.

To the many doctors, nurses, physical therapists and caregivers who have been a part of my recovery, I recognize and understand that you literally saved my life and helped me progress. Because of your incredible talents and love for my family, it made it easier for me to win the mental battles. I even remember very busy doctors coming to our house on their own time just to check on my well-being.

I need to recognize a few individuals who have specifically helped me on this book. Karleen Andresen is my mentor who has pushed me, taught me and always seen through my clouds of doubt and laid her eyes upon the true potential in sharing my story. Also, for Jason Wright's knowledgeable advice when I needed direction.

Most importantly, I must humbly acknowledge that without the love and sacrifice of the Savior in my life, I would be lost, assuming I would still be here at all. Being able to sincerely pray to a Father in Heaven during my moments of despair gives me hope and peace when it's nowhere else to be found. Knowing that my family can be together forever inspires my soul to be better, try harder, and serve more. Divine intervention has played a critical role in my life so far and I fully believe that will continue for me, just as it can for you.

Foreword

Nathan Ogden has lived up to his word that he would write a book to inspire others to be more and do more with what God has given them, regardless of their circumstances.

I remember the first thing Dad [Zig Ziglar] noticed about Nathan when he rolled into our greenroom at the Get Motivated conference in Boise, Idaho back in 2009 was that he had done an excellent job in "marrying up"! Nathan's beautiful and bright wife, Heather, was, as she still is, confidently by his side.

Our visit could not have lasted more than 20 minutes, and Nathan and Heather made such a positive impression on me, Mom and Dad, that I asked Nathan to please let me read his book before he got it published. I was my father's editor for twenty years and I wanted to help the young man whose passion was to help others. Nathan's outlook and attitude reminded me strongly of my father's own determination to continue encouraging folks after he suffered a traumatic brain injury and short term memory loss in 2007.

I am more than impressed with Nathan Ogden's inspiring and instructive book *UNFROZEN*.

My father often spoke of how important it is to offer solutions to the great trials and tribulations of life. Many can tell a good story, but few have done the hard work of learning how to convey the solutions they discovered to others in a way that allows them to apply those solution to their own lives.

Nathan has accomplished what few can or do. His story is beautifully and powerfully written. It is also 100% applicable! Every area of life that challenged him has been shared with his reader with great personal transparency, and for that I applaud him. I took notes for myself all the way through, and I will cherish and apply what Nathan has taught me in the years ahead.

I am honored to endorse this powerful, life changing, life improving, book. *Unfrozen* will move you forward in life, love, gratitude and relationships. I encourage you to "seize the moment" and let Nathan's book help you see what it is to truly keep moving boldly toward your future.

Julie Ziglar Norman

Table of Contents

"Go ahead Andrew, I'll see you when I land. This is going to be awesome!" I say, anxiously standing in line.

I haven't gone off a ski jump this big in a long time.

Snowflakes floating down the front of my old red goggles obscure my view as I visualize the approach to this twelve-foot-wide snow mound. The tall skier in front of me pushes off. As his descent begins, I squint to focus on the route he chooses.

Andrew's bright green jacket catches the corner of my eye as he meets up with a small group of skiers and snowboarders. They're watching others attempt big air and new tricks off a man-made jump halfway up the powdered covered peaks of Mount Bachelor ski resort, just outside of Bend, Oregon.

The skier ahead of me slows down just before contact and jumps off the right side closest to the crowd. He soars through the air before touching down to continue his further descent towards the warm lodge.

"It's my turn—am I ready for this?" I think to myself as I slide into position standing sideways in the snow, forty yards uphill from the jump.

"It's not too late to back out. Nobody up here knows who I am."

The pressure begins to build as others are waiting in line. My internal battle continues. "I've been skiing my whole life. I've told my brother-in-law that I was a good skier—now is my chance to prove it."

"Hurry up!" Someone yells from the line of excited adventurers behind me.

"Let's see what you've got."

I bend my knees and then spring into the air while pivoting both legs downhill, directing my newly waxed skis straight into the steep run. Digging my poles in the snow, I thrust myself forward toward my target.

As my perspective shifts and my velocity increases, I realize it's much larger than I thought.

I slow down as fear creeps into my mind, commanding my full attention. The fear of messing up, the fear of getting hurt, but most of all, the fear of looking foolish. Then the adrenaline kicks in and I move swiftly past confident to cocky.

"I've got this! I'm going to go bigger and better than anyone else here and they will all be in awe."

I pull my skis tightly together for the last fifteen yards, now hurling down the hill and aiming directly at the middle of the giant drift of packed snow.

As the back of my skis leave the top of the intimidating jump launching me skyward, I hear faint gasps from those gathered to watch. I instantly know something is wrong. I'm off balance as my body keeps climbing higher in the thin mountain air. Not ten, not twenty, but 30 feet above the snow packed slope I reach the pinnacle of my flight as my body rotates backwards.

My back faces the ground with my ski tips pointing straight in the air. For a moment I feel as if there is no gravity at all gazing at the puffy white clouds floating in the sky above me. Amidst all of this, I recognize the gentle touch of a snowflake on my uncovered cheek as everything goes into slow motion.

Looking to my right I see skiers watching me take flight through the lightly scratched lenses of my goggles.

Suddenly, gravity grabs ahold of me and I am quickly forced back to Earth. "This is really going to hurt," I think. "Maybe this is one of those dreams where you wake up right before you hit the ground." (It's truly amazing how many thoughts rush through your mind in a time like this.)

The inevitable force of the impact feels as though I have been dropped from an airplane holding nothing but a cocktail umbrella to slow me down. I slam head first into the frozen mountain with the full weight of my 180-pound body crushing down on my neck like an accordion. I violently tumble down the hill, rolling out of control until sliding to a stop, facing downhill on my right side in the fetal position. My skis, poles and gloves are all scattered far from my limp body.

I slowly open my eyes to get a visual perspective of the scene around me. My first thoughts are not concern for my well-being, but rather perception of me. I immediately think, "I look stupid and need to get up. I've really embarrassed myself in front of everyone watching. What an idiot."

I try to sit up, but only my left elbow raises moving slowly into the air and then immediately falling back to the packed snow. "That's okay, no big deal. I just knocked the wind out of myself. Just wait a few moments and I'll be back to normal," I assure myself.

I try again but this time my elbow only raises half as high as the first attempt.

Faint voices are getting closer. My forehead is stinging from smacking the snow, so I reach up to adjust my stocking hat.

Now my arm won't move at all.

An intense burning pain resonates throughout my whole body, as if I were laying on an open fire pit, burning alive. My breaths shorten and I realize I am struggling to breathe! I feel an immense pressure squeezing the life out of my lungs. I glance down at my legs stacked one on top of the other. Thoughts begin racing through my mind. "Why aren't they moving? What has happened to me? What about my wife and kids? How can I fix this?"

I'm frozen. I know something serious has happened, but I can't conceive the severity of my injuries in that moment. I never imagined later that day I would be told I was paralyzed.

And I never would have dreamed I'd be told that twice.

1

The Arctic Storm

*"What you get by achieving your goals
is not as important as what you become
by achieving your goals."*
—ZIG ZIGLAR

WHEN LIFE HITS YOU SQUARE IN THE JAW, you are
confused. While taking in your surroundings, trying
to piece together a plan of action, your ears are still
ringing from the impact. What just happened—is this
for real? I hurt all over. I can't deal with this right now.
I'm scared and don't know what to do.

It's okay to be confused in these situations. It's
perfectly normal not to have an answer when asked,
"What do we do now?" I know I didn't, and I still don't
have all of the answers. Choices I make for one situation
don't always work on another. It's an ongoing process
that if you want to succeed, you must continually make

purpose filled choices that allow you to move forward. Even if it's just making the decision that you won't give up. This is a step forward and that gives you a direction to go.

Deep emotional injuries, feeling completely broken inside and wanting to quit, have been companions of mine for some time. My life was mirroring perfection until I was abruptly blindsided and thrown into a world I had only heard of, but never thought I'd experience. I couldn't imagine this nightmare would ever happen to me. We never do.

Born and raised in Boise, Idaho, to a loving family, I held the title of middle child out of five energetic kids. Being actively involved in sports, church, school and the outdoors was just a way of life for me. If I wasn't hiking somewhere in the mountains, I was competing athletically on a team. After serving a two-year mission in Cleveland, Ohio, for The Church of Jesus Christ of Latter-day Saints, I met an amazing woman during my second year of college.

Heather was beautiful, adventurous, athletic, smart and funny. Heads turned as she walked in a room and traced her every move. Our brief friendship turned to romance as we dated for one fabulous month. Our whirlwind engagement breezed by the next month and the out-of-my-league girl made me explode with excitement as we vowed to stay together for eternity.

We were married in Portland, Oregon. The luckiest man alive with my bride by my side.

Our family picture — Summer of 2001
Nathan 26, Heather 23, Seniya 2 yrs, Kyler 7 mths

Over the next few years I earned a college degree, we bought our first home, were blessed with two children and my career had momentum. At 26 years of age, my aspirations started taking hold and the future held bright possibilities.

21

As the year 2001 neared its end, just three days before Christmas, we traveled to Bend, Oregon, to celebrate the holiday with Heather's family. My future forever changed as I launched myself off that fateful ski jump at Mt. Bachelor. I suffered an incomplete cervical spine fracture and spinal cord injury at the level of C7.

Family fun in the hospital

The next year I spent fighting to survive a number of serious health complications and striving to become as strong as possible. You're told in the hospital after a spinal cord injury, "If you're going to regain any physical movement it will most likely happen during a two-year window. The majority of your return, however, will take place in the first few months to a year."

I worked painstakingly hard each day, experiencing difficult physical therapy with excruciating pain. Any idea or cutting edge therapy that was available, I gave it my all — *anything* to increase the possibility of walking again. During the first year of my recovery from the neck break, I regained full use of my shoulders, arms, most of my hands, and a tiny bit in my legs. Even though only small movement came from my lower extremities, they were moving. I knew that as long as I kept progressing, I could do this! My life may have called for an intermission, but we would be back to our normal life before the next season's snow flew.

Having a truck equipped with hand controls, I could now drive, giving me the freedom to go where I wanted to go and not where someone else decided to drop me off. In most cases you see someone in a wheelchair and you immediately think, *minivan.* No matter what my future held, I would not allow my truck to be traded in for a "mom-van." The vehicle with new technology allowed me to drive to work each day and start providing for my family again like a good husband and father should.

Though a little different, our young family was getting back on track. We had a comfortable home, two wonderful children, a stable job and our dreams were still intact. The "ice" began to melt around my progression and each day I felt more and more unfrozen. My life started gently flowing forward like a mountain stream, gradually getting bigger and gaining speed as goals were accomplished and new dreams became reality.

During those 13 months, I had recovered almost 50% of my body movement and was filled with a powerful optimism about the endless possibilities. My body was starting to move more, but I still struggled with other health issues not as easy to see on the surface.

Due to the paralysis, my lungs and diaphragm were compromised, leaving me more exposed to certain illnesses, and I contracted a severe case of pneumonia. My blood-to-oxygen level dropped too low one night and I went unconscious in my sleep. Heather was unable to wake me early that morning and desperately called an ambulance. While in the ER, and still completely unconscious, I fell off the X-ray table and broke my neck — *again*. This break was higher up at the C6 level. I instantly lost the use of my hands, triceps and any movement in my legs I had recovered over the past year.

After I regained consciousness, my wife lovingly explained what had occurred that morning while we waited alone in an empty cold hospital room. When Heather was done speaking, three words immediately came to my mind, and I softly spoke to my wife, "Bring it on."

We had done this once before and we could do it again.

It's better that this happen two times to me than just once to someone else. We know what we're doing and we can accomplish it faster and more efficient this time.

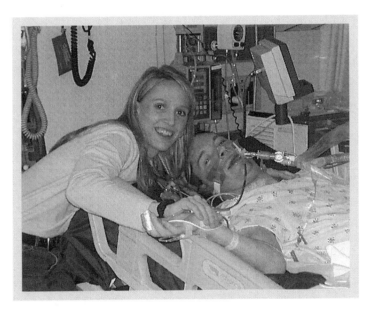

My second neck break in the x-ray room Feb. 4, 2003
"Bring it on"

Shortly after my second neck surgery, I pushed full steam ahead.

"I need to get back everything I had worked so hard for. I am still going to walk again and this setback will not alter that goal," I told myself.

A few weeks into this new battle, a frustrating realization became crystal clear to me, but I didn't want to see it. All of the movement and abilities I had lost falling from the X-ray table were not coming back. I was stuck and unable to move. I couldn't accept this halt in my progress. What about my dreams? There was far too much left for me to accomplish that I needed my legs and hands for. So many adventures I wanted to feel and experience from a standing position. I need to work harder, or pray with greater faith — that will be my breakthrough giving me momentum again.

As much as I've tried over the years, the sought-after physical movement I lost on that fateful early morning in the emergency room still hasn't returned to accompany me.

Life can be hard! It can be paralyzing and make you feel powerless! I fought so hard to progress that far in my recovery only to have it ripped out from under me. After the second neck break I was not only suffering from another physical impairment but was agonizing about my future mentally as well. So many others looked up to me as their example of strength and courage by how I've handled these situations.

I asked myself, *"Am I strong enough to keep pushing forward? What do I do now? How do I keep the hope and faith that everything will be all right? I still want to walk again!"*

Life is an endless process to *become* someone. A business is compiled of dozens, hundreds, or even thousands of smaller processes that must thread together to deliver a finished product into the customer's hands. Anything from creation, research and development, marketing, billing, human resources, sales, shipping and management. Each of these departments can be filled with dozens of tiny procedures of their own. If any one of these tasks is not completed correctly, the company as a whole could suffer great losses or setbacks. This slows down their progress of *becoming* what they envisioned. If your research and development department is not inventing the best product that can be sold for a competitive price, the competition will create it and take over your market share.

It's no different in your personal life. You are a product that is being sold to the public. Everyone you come in contact with each day is watching and making a decision. Will they want to become a friend or colleague with the person they see, or will they move onto the next aisle in search of something of a different variety? Every experience you have and every choice you make is molding you into the person you are *becoming*. Are your choices creating the person you want to be, in the life you want to live?

You might think you didn't want to become the person you are today. When you were younger you had a whole different plan in mind of what you would be when you grew up. You didn't choose this life and the struggles you've faced. That's out of your control, right?

There is a lot of truth to that. We don't always choose the trials we've had to endure. However, we have made relevant decisions during those trials that are continually shaping ourselves into what others see, and more importantly, what we see in ourselves.

Who do you want to become, and what steps will it take to get there? If you want to be known as an honest person that consistently tells the truth, no matter how uncomfortable and embarrassing the consequence, you can choose to do that. If your dream is to live a long happy life married to the same person, then put your spouse's needs first and never let your eyes wander. If being financially successful is your goal, then put in the energy, sacrifice and hard work ethic so you can attain that dream.

When you know where you want to end up, then it helps to create a roadmap of what you must do to get there. The path we take in this life is rarely the one we hoped for. There will be roadblocks, disasters and even sinkholes that will make you feel your desired path is no longer available.

Zig Ziglar put it best when he said, *"When obstacles arise, you change your direction to reach your goal, you do not change your decision to get there."*

Sitting at home with a second crippling broken neck was devastating. I was staring at the realization that I would most likely never stand up taller than my wife again. There would be no need for her to get on her tippy toes to kiss me. Now I will always look up to her.

Imagine all the activities you use your fingers for each day that make you productive and happy. Playing the piano was so inspiring and relaxing to me when the pressures of life weighed heavy on my shoulders. That peaceful remedy had now vanished. Throwing a tennis ball into a local pond for my black lab, Sage — one of my best friends — was no longer an option. I particularly loved bending over and holding hands with my 2-year-old daughter before church. She felt like a princess in her pretty white dress and ponytails as we danced around the family room together in our pretend castle. Truth be told, she made me feel more special than I ever did her.

Of course there's much more to it than this, but these are some of the little joys in life I will miss. All these tiny snippets of wonder are now gone and I can't choose to bring them back. Only through my mind's eye will I re-live these very ordinary experiences that have now become extraordinary memories.

Now what? Do I quit and let others run my life because it's too hard, or do I push forward?

I stumbled through every emotion imaginable, from feeling completely indestructible to a brief thought of suicide. Hopelessness, remorse, resentment and despair, were all invited to my party. On the surface everyone saw a very positive and driven individual who wouldn't give up. Deep down I'm not sure if anyone, even my wife, knew the terrifying doubt and fear I was suppressing.

"This is not who I wanted to be. People expect more of me. I expect more of me." Though I felt a great deal of loss, I never did lose one thing — my faith. Faith that life could be better. Faith that I can do more. Faith that I can *become* the person I've always envisioned.

I'm not saying that all pain, suffering, and feelings of despair have good that come from them. I don't believe this to be true. There are terrible acts of destruction to the mind, body, and spirit out there. I do believe that even though these instances may occur, there is an opportunity for growth and strength to come from them. Making the most of these experiences can be extremely difficult and challenging to comprehend. It is up to you to sift through the rubble, find the good, and decide to apply those learned principles in your life.

Months passed by and we continued with our family motto of "We Believe." These two words were written on a large piece of poster board and hung on the wall of every hospital or therapy room I stayed. As I regained strength, Heather and I decided to finish a goal we had always desired. By using the help of doctors, and without telling anyone of our strategy, Heather got pregnant with our third child through intra-uterine insemination. We had always wanted to have four children and my wife was brave enough, or some say crazy enough, to keep working on this dream. Our little girl, Malani, brought so much happiness to our young family, which made me crave for more progress.

Then two years later our youngest child, Cortlyn, entered this world, with no medical help, reaching our goal of the four children, that we had always stayed up late talking about as newlyweds. What a spectacular blessing these two girls have been in our lives. One of our dreams became a reality because we changed our direction to get there, but not the goal.

Life hit me square in the jaw and it hurt. It hurt bad! Not many people will break their neck on two separate occasions, leaving more of their body paralyzed each time. I came to realize this was all part of my purpose, that there was a mission I needed to accomplish. What that mission is, has been an ongoing process to discover.

What are your aspirations in life, and are you on track to accomplish them? Don't expect this transformation of becoming who you desire, to happen overnight. It takes time and discipline to change thoughts and behavior. Always be willing to say, "Bring it on," because you are capable of greatness, and no one can generate this forward momentum but you. You must believe in yourself and have faith that your life will become everything you've ever dreamed of. It's time to live a life *unfrozen*!

CHAPTER QUESTIONS:

What life-changing event has blindsided me?

_____

_____

_____

_____

_____

What empowering traits have I acquired while
overcoming this trial?

_____

_____

_____

_____

_____

Who do I want to _become_ and why?

_____

_____

_____

_____

_____

_____

What three changes will I make in my life to get there?

_____

_____

_____

_____

_____

2

Chipping Away At Excuses

"Excuses are lies we tell ourselves so that it doesn't have to be our fault."
—UNKNOWN

I'VE BEEN AN AVID USER OF EXCUSES and have applied them long before I was paralyzed. Sitting in a wheelchair just took those opportunities to an entirely new level.

So what are excuses and why do we use them? An excuse is "an explanation given to defend or justify an act or offense."

When we do something wrong we usually know it's wrong and are already making up an excuse in our head. In our minds we want to believe that others don't think poorly of us. It doesn't matter if we have to blame others as long as we don't look bad. By mentioning an excuse we are hoping, and sometimes expecting, others to overlook or forgive the results of our actions. The following experience took place when I was just starting out in business and has stuck with me ever since.

Recalling back to my pre-wheel years, I was the acting station manager of a worldwide delivery company, managing 15 employees and also overseeing the day-to-day operations of the state I lived in. In the delivery industry, everything is recorded and extremely time sensitive. Profits and losses depend on it. My group was productive, on time, motivated and almost always met our goals. From the outside, we were a stellar team that other teams pined to be a part of.

One member of our team, I'll call Tina, had a large family and seemed to genuinely care about her children. Tina doted over them, telling the team great stories about their successes and accolades, and she required a high level of performance from them. However, Tina danced to a different genre and held herself to unequal levels. Arriving daily with wrinkled attire, an un-tucked shirt, mismatched socks and an overall unkempt appearance. You could catch Tina out around the corners surrounded by tobacco-filled clouds, wafting the trail of her last puff into the office. What she lacked in hygiene was not balanced by her social skills.

As a manager, this was not an ideal representative for our stellar team and company appearance, but may be overlooked if their job performance exceeded expectations and the deliveries were made on time.

Even though she worked at the company longer than me, I had been morphed into one of those situations where I became the boss and she felt passed up. Any time a junior takes leadership over an established employee, there is bound to be contention. But I kept my focus on the team and their proficiency. It came time for her annual performance review and to be honest, I wasn't very excited to give it.

When I conducted the review, it included stats on delivery, execution of delivery, reliability, process of distribution, vehicle maintenance and driving record—how many stops and what types of stops the team member makes. I was fortunate: The company's data system was intense and comprehensive. I literally knew every move she made and when she made it. I also gathered any information I could on the cohesiveness of her team and how she contributed to their efficiency.

The annual review was scheduled. To prepare, I gathered all the needed current data as well as data from the last performance review. On paper, Tina seemed an average worker, hitting acceptable outcomes and worth retaining as a team member.

On review day, she came in with a chip on her shoulder, giving me the sense she was posturing for battle. She wanted to fight but for the wrong reasons. She was meeting goals. She knew her job. She could put her head down and follow through. The problem that came up repeatedly with Tina was excuses. I'm not talking about unique and unexpected excuses. I'm talking about the situations we all have control over. In one 30-day period, Tina was late seven times: her children were sick a couple different days, her husband lost his keys, which delayed her, she had a doctor's appointment, and her car broke down three times. These were excuses often repeated each month.

Handing a manager a circumstance like this created a trickle-down effect. When she was late, packages got delayed and others took on a heavier load to compensate. This provoked her peers to make comments and created tension within the team. It caused disruption, negativity and disintegration of morale. That became a company problem and they expected me to take action.

———

"If you really want to do something, you will find a way. If you don't, you'll find an excuse."

— JIM ROHN, author and motivational speaker

———

During our review that morning I was on the fence of whether to keep her or let her go. If she was willing to make some changes with her attitude and accountability, I was more than willing to work with Tina and help her succeed. The company invested a great deal of money and time into her over the last five years and didn't want to see her go. Throughout the 45-minute discussion, a disappointing decision had been made. Sadly she packed up her locker and headed out the door for the last time. I wished her well, but couldn't ignore the blatant issue. She failed to take responsibility for her lack of actions that kept her from progressing.

Progress is about moving forward. If Tina recognized the hurdles happening in her life, she could have created a backup plan, allowing her to keep moving forward in her personal and professional life. Like on the job, Tina saw these as excuses, things outside her control, situations that life was throwing at her. Since it was life that was "causing" these constant problems, then she merely expected everyone else to accept the justifications she constantly made. In her mind, who are we to question her decisions, we would have done the same thing. I know this because I've done it myself.

Why do we do this to ourselves? Why don't we just choose what's best for us each time so we don't have to keep going through this? It all comes down to one word — fear. Fear of the unknown makes us wonder what might happen if we don't get our desired results.

All of us are scared to some degree—it's human nature. We are afraid of pain, embarrassment, retribution, responsibility, failure and even scared of success. Doesn't that sound crazy to be scared of success? It's a very real fear though. It starts off as a salesman striving to be outstanding at their job and a top performer in that field.

> More clients = more money =
> bigger house and more toys =
> more notoriety = more happiness.

Right? As this dream begins taking shape, we start to notice the reality of that success.

> More clients = more travel =
> less T-ball games = less choir concerts =
> less waking up next to your spouse =
> less happiness.

That doesn't mean you shouldn't strive to magnify your talents and become the absolute best in wherever your desires lead you. Of course you should. Just remember we can only physically be in one place at a time.

In addition to all these fears, we are brutally attacked with guilt, disappointment and regret. These three words carry heavy weight, almost like a cement block around your neck while swimming. Regret of "what could have been" and "opportunities lost" is not easily dismissed or forgiven.

How many times have you wanted to say you're sorry but couldn't bring yourself to do it, wanted to ask for forgiveness but let the moment slip by, allowed your nerves to get the best of you when longing to ask that special person on a date. I know I have many times. We try to tell ourselves it doesn't really matter, but deep down inside, we know it does.

Fear of the unknown makes us wonder what might happen if we don't get our desired results.

The fear we are battling is really a fear of progress. Any progress at all, but in particular the kind of progress you really want and deserve to experience. Without progress in life, we feel insignificant, unimportant—almost invisible. We lose hope. So we attach blame and start pointing fingers at others.

"Why am I still stuck here? Who didn't do their part so I can be where I should be? It can't be my fault."

Most of the time the problem is ourselves. We are the ones holding us back from reaching our full potential. Not your boss, family, teacher, coach, or even your health. Here are some examples of different excuses that you may have heard before, or maybe even used:

- ❖ I'm too busy for that.
- ❖ I'd like too, but I'm not as qualified as them.
- ❖ It's too hard.
- ❖ I'm addicted to something.

- ❖ I can't, I come from a poor background.
- ❖ I'm a single parent, you don't understand.
- ❖ I'm too old, overweight, not smart enough.
- ❖ This is as good as I can do.
- ❖ I'm just not lucky enough.
- ❖ I'm just too scared.

I like to call this your trump card. In many card games there is a trump card or wild card. In UNO it would be the Draw Four Wild card. By playing this trump card you are saying that your card is more powerful than any other card on the table, so you win. You feel justified in playing the card wherever and whenever you decide, even if others disagree. We play this imaginary card in life when we're scared, need attention, or are being pushed out of our comfort zones. You know you do it. We all do. The question is: What card do you play?

The card I've pulled from my hand many times is what my wife and I dubbed the "Q card," or quadriplegic card. After my first paralyzing injury, I used sympathy, manipulation and a wide range of excuses as to why I wasn't able to do simple things. I convinced people to get me better seats, parking, rooms, backstage passes, and even bigger discounts for nothing extra on my part. I had others do my bidding to purchase products inside the store, gave a urine sample, and even drew blood for medical tests—all while sitting in my truck.

Impressive, huh? Sometimes I would even call another person and have them look up a phone number for me so I didn't have to struggle turning the pages in a phone book. (For those of you who are younger, a phone book is an actual heavy book that has thousands of numbers and addresses.) All of these activities I was capable of doing on my own but chose to rationalize the extra effort it would have taken. I told you I was the king of excuses.

I know exactly what it looks and feels like to play a trump card. My progress came to a halt and I started manipulating people's feelings and emotions to get what I wanted, or felt I deserved. I was more paralyzed mentally than my arms and legs combined, and that changed me. The active, go get-em, capable man my wife had grown to love and trust was fading away.

Why is progress so important? The act of moving forward, or progressing, builds faith and confidence. For an older man with a hip replacement to carefully walk across the room to his dresser, pick out a pair of socks, and slowly move back to the bed is huge. The next day he may venture out to the mailbox and then around the block because his confidence is increasing and turning into knowledge. Knowledge that he can do hard things.

Or a young woman going out to lunch with a friend for the first time since experiencing a devastating miscarriage is a giant step toward emotional healing. Even a tiny step initiates momentum in the right direction. Always remember that fear is the opposite of faith.

The Nathan who used to stand tall and get things done on his own was now slowly beginning to shrink and I didn't recognize him. No one else identified this dissent because they were blinded by my physical condition. Even if they did notice, who was going to tell a newly paralyzed man some of the choices he's making might be hurtful down the road? Overall, you begin to lose hope and surrender power. This is real paralysis and it comes from the inside out.

If you're under the impression this only happens to the weak-minded and doesn't apply to you, it's time to take a closer look at your life. Breaking free from emotional, spiritual, and mental paralysis is not a walk in the park — it's work. It can be as difficult as a quadriplegic completing a half triathlon.

Stopping the excuses begins with a few steps or reality checks:

1. Recognize the excuses.
2. Play it through.
3. Throw them out.

Recognize the excuses

First you must recognize you are making excuses, determine what they are, and that you have the control to change them. It may be something you've said for so long you don't even realize you're doing it. Take time to sit back and analyze your interactions with others and yourself. Do you really not have time to exercise and eat better, or do you just say that because you're scared of the effort and sacrifice that will be involved. Even though you know you'll be much happier if you hit the gym. Little adjustments made now will avoid a large justification created later. For Tina, it might have been a simple backup friend that could have driven her to work, scheduling a doctor with late office hours, or a new alarm clock.

~~~~~~~

Do you think enough of yourself to take a risk? If you believe you can do great things, you will.

~~~~~~~

Play it through

Another way is to play the current scenario all the way out in your mind. What will happen if you fail to accomplish that task? Will it really matter? Take your current situation and quickly, in your mind, create a short movie trailer of what might happen if you choose to apply to the college of your dreams, get that lump screened by a doctor, introduce yourself to the beautiful girl at the next table. What will happen if you choose not to? Your life won't be much different if that girl turns you down, but what if she ends up as your wife. Is the possible embarrassment worth that risk?

Many times we play our story to a certain point and then we stop. Like a kid stealing a piece of candy from the store. They picture their self eating their candy, the way it tastes and how they satisfied their desire. But did they think it all the way through? What they didn't anticipate was getting caught by their parents. What's the rest of the story? They most likely get in trouble, visit the store manager to tell them what happened, pay for it with money they may not have and lose some amount of trust. Knowing the rest of the story helps clear the vision and allows a new choice, a better option, a decision that may align more closely with your purpose. If they thought all the way through the scenario, would the child have taken the candy in the first place? Probably not.

~~~~~~

The results you desire may not be immediate, but they will only come as you exercise discipline and patience.

~~~~~~

If you think 10 minutes, 10 days, or even 10 years down the road what the consequence of that choice is, you may very well choose differently. You could end up with a better career, stronger family, and more peace and fulfillment in life.

Throw them out

The third step is to throw your trump cards away. Once you realize the alibi you've been telling is not empowering, but restricting, the easier it gets to not use. Don't get me wrong—it can be difficult. It will be uncomfortable, annoying, and eye opening. Though mentally and physically challenging, it is crucial to believe in yourself and your abilities. The results you desire may not be immediate, but they will only come as you exercise discipline and patience. Destroy those trump cards for good.

By throwing out some cards you are now left with at least one empty spot in your hand. Nobody wants someone to say, "they're a few cards short of a full deck." You don't have to worry though. The remarkable confidence and crucial memories gained from making these correct choices will fill these gaps and propel you forward with even greater strength to continue. It will become easier and easier each time because you're not dealing with as much guilt, disappointment, and remorse anymore. This process is empowering and helps you stand a little bit taller each day.

When we have to choose between where we are now or where we want to be, many times we put our heads down and pick now. Do you think enough of yourself to take a risk? If you believe you can do great things, you will. Excuses hold you back and stunt your growth. Your challenges could be as little as getting up on time or as big as adopting a new child. You must start one step at a time so it's not overwhelming and next thing you know you'll be on your way to becoming a new you, a better you.

"It's not the mountains ahead that wear you out, but the grain of sand in your shoe."

—UNKNOWN

The truth is we choose how we spend our time each day. The things you really want to do get done. The rest is lost to our excuses. One of my favorite quotes of all time hung on the wall in my father's office:

As you reach inside your shoe and pull out that grain of sand—your most-used excuse—think of the mountain peaks you'll climb in this life now that those irritants aren't constantly hurting and holding you back from obtaining your dreams.

CHAPTER QUESTIONS:

What "trump card" do I use the most?

_____

_____

_____

Why do I use this excuse?

_____

_____

_____

If I couldn't fail, what would I aspire to do?

_____

_____

_____

What 3 fears keep me from obtaining that dream?

_____

_____

_____

What will I do to conquer these fears and excuses?

_____

_____

_____

_____

3

~~~~~~~~~~~~~~~~~~~~~~~~~

Iced Over With Depression

"Growth is painful. Change is painful. But nothing is as painful as staying stuck somewhere you don't belong." —MANDY HALE

SOMETHING EXTREMELY DIFFICULT for others to understand, and nearly impossible to fully explain, is the dark abyss of feeling alone and worthless in this world. Being alone is one thing, but feeling alone can be entirely different.

You could be stranded on a small deserted island in the South Pacific for months and *be* completely alone. However, if you believe a ship is on its way, a rescue plane is just over the horizon, or even if an old volleyball named Wilson is your new best friend, you still possess something so powerful it can't be stopped. Hope! You may be so scared you're afraid to move, making you mentally paralyzed. No matter how dark your surroundings get, it's undeniable that hope is stronger than fear. Deep in your mind you believe there are others thinking of and trying to save you. You know in the end everything will be okay.

On the other hand, *feeling* alone can seem like a black hole sucking away everything good in your life, forever. Everyone has forgotten you, lied to you, doesn't understand your situation, and no one cares anymore. Every ounce of desire has been drained from your very being. On your own it seems insurmountable to gain your footing and climb out of this despair. Just *being* alone won't break you, but *knowing* you're alone can drive you insane. I have walked down this bumpy road in the past and seen terrifying places I will never forget.

Slowly I was learning to not always be rushing to the next activity but find the joy and happiness all around me, right now.

There is an unusually dark side of depression that includes things like suicide, abuse and extreme addictions. That kind of depression is reserved for the highest trained experts in counseling. I'm talking about depression that immobilizes your progress, the kind of depression that makes you lay in bed for days, or makes you manipulate people to do things so you don't have to.

Depression: What does it look like? How does it really feel?

After being paralyzed I quickly realized I had a tremendous amount of time to just sit and think. Yes, I do *a lot* of sitting. The act of slowing down taught me to appreciate the present while pondering the future. Those moments have been irreplaceable. I taught my young children more about how bees pollinate flowers and why airplanes fly in the sky because I was forced to stop and take it all in. Many of those little opportunities are lost because we get too busy and demand so much of ourselves.

Most of the time I never had a choice of where to go because the few muscles that did work in my arms were too weak to push a wheelchair. For quite a while I relied solely on someone else to go places.

At times my only mode of transportation was that little blonde girl with ponytails I used to dance with in our living room. She was constantly seen pushing my wheelchair around the neighborhood, sometimes with me in it. This allowed me to experience more of life than sitting in the house or a doctor's office.

Occasionally we brought 3-year-old Kyler along, sitting on my lap and loving the adventure. We had so much fun together. Me, teaching with my words, and them, learning and living with their legs. I just knew a third neck break was immanent as Seniya would accidentally steer the chair off the sidewalk, causing me to fall into the road. I was never seriously hurt but it was kind of dangerous. Heather didn't approve of our actions, so we would have to sneak out of the house sometimes to go on our fun walks. What an amazing young daredevil the Lord blessed me with. Slowly I was learning to not always be rushing to the next activity but find the joy and happiness all around me, right now.

However, when your mind slows down for too long, an extremely dangerous transformation begins to take place. This is when pain, doubt, loneliness and despair start to sneak into your life. Most of the time we don't recognize it's even happening until it's started grabbing control of our life. There were moments I was stuck all by myself facing one direction with no way of turning my wheelchair, or even my head because of the metal halo. Staring at a blank wall in the hospital for 25 minutes while my wife talks to the doctors was frustrating to say the least.

What do you think about when the view never changes and you're wondering if you have any self worth?

There were many painful emotions demanding my attention, so I began asking some of these tough questions. "Why does life have to be so hard? Why can't I ever get a break? Nobody really cares about me and what I'm going through. Why does everything happen to me?"

All this was very new to me and I didn't know what was going on. If only I was educated and humble enough to recognize that many of the little choices I was making were throwing up red flags everywhere. If only I could have blocked these feelings out, I could have stopped traveling down the slippery slide to feeling depressed.

I don't want this to happen to you, so here are a few of the symptoms of depression from WebMD to look for in yourself or someone else:

- ❖ Inescapable sadness
- ❖ No motivation
- ❖ Unexplained weight loss or gain
- ❖ Insomnia or extreme sleepiness
- ❖ Fatigue
- ❖ Feeling guilt or worthlessness
- ❖ Lack of concentration
- ❖ Suicidal thoughts
- ❖ Decreased interest in activities
- ❖ Irritability or anger

All of these signs will not be present in every person but some of them fit me like a glove. Not too long after the second neck break, some of these symptoms began inching into my life. I wasn't paying attention and the process was so slow I'm not sure I would've recognized it anyway.

I desperately tried to be a good husband and father but was slipping into depression and denial. I was still actively involved in the family because I would go outside with the kids to play or support them during their sports games. We went to parties, on family vacations and I held a few temporary jobs. In looking back, though, I realize I was physically there but mentally staring into space wishing I was in bed.

My goal was to start a motivational speaking company. I had big plans on how many people I would help and how successful I could be. Waking up each morning I was truly excited to make tremendous progression toward this ambition as I entered my home office ready to work. Hours later, very little had been accomplished while I stared at the computer screen. It wasn't that I didn't want to or wasn't willing to—I just *couldn't*. Because of this I wasn't providing for my family like I should.

I wanted to do more but constantly thought of laying in bed. At least being in bed felt like the severe physical and emotional pain wasn't as strong. I didn't have to put on a fake smile and act like everything was just fine. So any moment I could justify being there, was well worth the effort. I never admitted it to others, but I fought endless suffocating feelings every day about not being able to walk again.

I often thought my life would never be the same. Do I really want this new life; how do I get excited about it?

I promised Heather, my loving and trusting companion, time and time again that things would change. That I would change. And I truly meant it! I promised to provide for the family better, to live healthier so she didn't worry I might die sooner, to be a better husband and father, and to fulfill my life's mission and motivate others. On many occasions there was continuous forward movement in my actions that lasted as long as a couple of months. Only to fall back into this black hole of lifelessness. I was living life with no meaningful progress and I hated it. Even my kids would tell me that I didn't laugh anymore, and they never saw me cry. There was somebody else living in my body.

The heartfelt promises I made to my dear wife had been broken and it was crushing our marriage. She felt like I had been unfaithful to her, and I guess she was right. I wasn't fulfilling my promises. It was almost like watching a car accident. I could see it happening right in front of me and desperately wanted to stop the damage about to happen, but for some reason I couldn't change the outcome.

I felt so much guilt and regret it was hard to breathe. I will never forget the thoughts imprinted across my mind:

"My wife deserves someone better than me. Our kids need a father more involved and in control. How will I ever achieve anything in life now? So many people look up to me, but I feel like a fraud."

I was highly sensitive to the belief that I had failed spiritually. That through these two neck breaks I had a special mission to touch and inspire others to face their challenges and fears. By procrastinating and not achieving this goal I felt inadequate and defeated. I let so many people down. I was depressed and it lasted for years. It's deafening to live with the guilt, remorse and embarrassment.

One of the most meaningful lessons I've learned is that there is no Superman. When you meet someone with impeccable hair, amazing job, beautiful wife and family, able to fly, looks good in tights, and seems perfect in every way—they're not real. Stop! Everyone, and I mean *everyone*, has their own kryptonite. It weakens your power to fight and diminishes your mental abilities to focus and act on your desires. Some weaknesses are more transparent, while others hide them deep inside. Many may not even know what's freezing their progress when it's right in front of their eyes.

Depression is a very treatable condition, not a disease or incurable illness. Now let's discuss some systems to combat the different aspects of depression in the next chapter.

CHAPTER QUESTIONS:

Am I depressed? What am I depressed about? (*Really think about it.*)

_____

_____

_____

What is the cause of my doubts and fears? (*Now think deeper than before.*)

_____

_____

_____

Do I truly believe I can recover, be healed, and move forward?

_____

_____

_____

If I read the next chapter will I receive
powerful tools to help me?

Of course I will!

4

Melting Depression

"At some point you just have to let go of what you thought should happen and live in what is happening."
— HEATHER HEPLER

THERE ARE MANY TECHNIQUES TO HELP SOMEONE struggling with anxiety, depression and pain. The following are six systems that help me. I don't say the word "helped" in the past tense, because I continue to climb this mountain every day. I know these techniques have value because I've tried them and they work.

Here are my favorite 6 systems to move from paralysis to progress:

1. Communication
2. Make a Decision
3. Service
4. Laugh
5. Touch
6. Therapy

1. Communication

"The quality of your life is the quality of your communication, with yourself as well as with others."

—ANTHONY ROBBINS

The first step in the healing process is to recognize that healing needs to take place. This happens through communication. Communicating with others and most importantly with yourself. It's tough to accept the fact that you're suffering from depression or anxiety. And even if we do admit it, most of us are too prideful to invest the time and energy to treat it. Nobody wants to feel like they don't have control, and that's exactly what depression will do.

It can make you want to hide from the world and disappear. But you know what? That's okay. It's natural to feel this way. The important thing is to not let it control you. If you want to sit on the couch all day watching TV with the blinds closed, go for it! Or lay in bed wallowing in your sorrows and tears, have at it! It's all right to take some time out, just give yourself a time limit. After one movie, one day, or one week, you must say to yourself, "This experience has been difficult, but I'm over it!" Then it's time to do something productive that will improve your mood.

Now that you've recognized there is a problem, you need to do what can be one of the most difficult aspects of the healing process. Communicate what you're thinking and feeling with others. Wow! That was hard just writing it, let alone doing it. I'm personally getting much better at doing this now, but for years I was terrible. I mean utterly horrendous—just ask my wife!

Disguising my true emotions and thoughts became a new pastime for me. Because I didn't want to worry others I began hiding most of my pain and fear. I thought that I was protecting my wife and family by pushing extreme doubt and fear deep inside my soul. I didn't want to worry them more than I already had. I wish now that I would've allowed those around me to know what I was really going through. They could have piled behind my truck and pushed me out of the deep muddy hole I was spinning my tires in. I needed their help, but wouldn't humble myself enough to convey what I needed.

This doesn't mean you need to pull out a ladder and scream from the rooftops that you have a problem. Nobody wants to do that. You should, however, express your feelings to someone. Family, friend, counselor, or even a stranger. It can be much easier to openly discuss your true emotions with a total stranger than someone who already knows you. Many of the barriers we normally put up to protect ourselves aren't in place yet. Typically a stranger isn't going to be one of your strongest supporters, though, but can be a good listener. Find someone you can trust and start talking.

This may be one of the hardest acts you've ever had to do in your life. Take the uncertainty and fear, take your trump card, and get rid of it. You can't start the healing process without opening up and communicating your feelings and needs with those that can help you.

Here is a little tip on how to focus your thoughts so you can get some forward momentum going. If you feel extremely awful, give that awfulness a name.

Frustrated? Mad? Lonely?

At least you're feeling something, and now you know what it is. Write it down in a notebook or journal. Yes, write it down. This may sound simple and insignificant, but we know suppressing our emotions doesn't work, so give it a try.

When you're not making decisions, you're not making progress.

This activity helps define what you're feeling, instead of letting your mind run wild without any parameters. Describing an emotion in just a word or two, helps reduce the negative emotion. You are now communicating in a positive way with yourself, and that triggers your mind into wanting more of that feeling. Now there is less unknown in life, which gives you more control.

2. Make a decision

"It doesn't matter which side of the fence you get off on sometimes. What matters most is getting off. You cannot make progress without making decisions." — JIM ROHN

It can be difficult to climb out of the hole you're in when you have no motivation or direction. That's why it's so critical to *just make a decision.* Any decision! It doesn't matter how big or small, but I would recommend starting small. When you're not making decisions, you're not making progress. When you're not making some kind of progress, you'll never gain the confidence needed to change and succeed.

Even if you haven't done anything to accomplish what you decided, you did do something. You made a choice.

Have you ever made a decision and almost immediately felt more relaxed and focused? Of course you have. Even if you haven't done anything to accomplish what you decided, you did do something. You made a choice. The act of just making a decision helps reduce worry and anxiety. You are progressing now and that feels good. Try getting out of bed and taking a shower, telling the truth all day long, or calling a close friend just to talk. You can now build upon that positive emotion and choose to do something else. Don't allow much time to pass in between each decision, or you're permitting negative thoughts to creep back into your mind.

Where we make a mistake is trying to get our choices correct 100% of the time. We don't want to mess up anymore because we're already extremely fragile. So when you're making your next decision, remember this quote, *"Done is better than perfect."* Trying to be perfect can cause extra stress and unneeded doubt. Does it really matter whether you wear a red blouse or a blue one? Probably not. Just completing any goal, whether it was perfect or not, empowers you to feel like you're in control and capable of doing much more.

By making decisions, you are proving to yourself that you are worth something. It may not seem like much, but you are mentally setting goals and preparing a plan to achieve them. Even if they're not written down, you will still see an increase in the quality of your life and a boost in your confidence. All of this creates an excitement to attain what you truly desire. Just start by making a decision.

3. Service

"Too often we underestimate the power of a touch, a smile, a kind word, a listening ear, an honest compliment, or

the smallest act of caring, all of which have the potential to turn a life around." —LEO BUSCAGLIA

According to the National Science Foundation, we have between 12,000 and 50,000 thoughts each day, and therapist H. Norman Wright says 75% of them are negative. Are you kidding me? Can you imagine tens of thousands of people coming up to you each day, tapping you on the shoulder and telling you something negative? A large portion of those thoughts would be something directed towards you personally. This could make you feel absolutely worthless, especially for those already swimming in the deep end of the pool with heavy insecurities wrapped around their neck. We need something to fight back with and serving others is a surefire way to curb those negative thoughts.

Serving those around you will be one of your greatest tools in fighting depression and other related conditions. The ability to focus on others' well-being and put energy toward *their* happiness positions you for an extraordinary comeback. It's not easy, but once the process has begun and you're *becoming* a better you, then all the peace and joy you desire will become reality.

There are 3 basic principles that must take place before one can give service at their full capacity.

1. Love
2. Forgiveness
3. Gratitude

To emphasize just how important love fits into the equation, we just have to look to the scriptures. The apostle Matthew recorded the Savior's humble reply to the Pharisees question, "Which is the great commandment in the law?"

"Jesus said unto him, Thou shalt love the Lord thy God with all thy heart, and with all thy soul, and with all thy mind.

"This is the first and great commandment.

"And the second is like unto it, Thou shalt love thy neighbor as thyself." —Matthew 22:37-39.

We must first have an unconditional love for our Father in Heaven. This love and guidance will provide the faith needed to begin loving yourself. As you begin gaining confidence and trust in your own self worth, it's a natural emotion to share that love with those around you. Love must be the foundation that creates lasting service. Then comes forgiveness.

Forgiving someone does not cancel out the consequences of their actions or relieve them of their moral responsibility. They still did something that hurt you. It is, however, vital to your emotional and spiritual progression. Forgiving others starts by forgiving ourselves from guilt and regret. Guilt can be a good thing when it encourages corrective action in our thoughts and behaviors. By letting go of the mistakes we've made, we can better empathize with the poor choices of others. Thus creating an atmosphere where a confident self-esteem can thrive and you can be grateful.

What are you grateful for? When you are miserable and have no motivation, the last thing you want to do is think about what you're grateful for. There is nothing to be grateful for, right? The cool thing is that it's not finding gratitude that is most important; it's remembering to search in the first place.

Are you grateful for your family, pet, house, good food, large campfires, soft pillows, fun music, or a favorite book? It doesn't matter if it's important to anyone else, just that it's important to you. Start a list right now. No, seriously, right now. List the first five things that pop into your mind. Jot down more in the columns if needed. Don't judge them or change them — they mean something special to you.

_____

_____

_____

_____

_____

Now that you are freely forgiving and finding gratitude, it's time to show it through your service. Consciously look for those in your workplace or neighborhood, especially in your home, to give of yourself and make their life easier.

"But it takes too much time and money. This can't be worth it," many might say.

Maybe they've never given of their time or means to lift another in need. The overwhelming feelings of gratification and fulfillment are unforgettable and highly rewarding. Help fix a flat tire for a family stranded on the side of the road. Put your arm around your daughter and dry her tears from a bad breakup. Assist in finishing a report for the coworker who procrastinated too long. Take a meal to the neighbors who just found out their son has cancer.

I vividly remember Heather walking into my hospital room to spend the evening with me the day I was flown back to Boise, Idaho. Tears came to her eyes as she humbly shared with me what it was like returning to our home after being gone for an extremely difficult three weeks. All of our Christmas decorations had been taken down and stored. The pantry, cupboards, and fridge were overflowing with frozen dinners, canned soups, diapers and even toothpaste. It wasn't just our family that provided these acts of service, it was our neighbors, church members, and even strangers that heard of what our family was going through and wanted to help. I will never forget how others stepped in and took care of my family when I wasn't physically and emotionally able to.

As you provide hope and comfort to everyone you're in contact with, an amazing transformation takes place. Your worries will seem modest and your dreams attainable. By serving others we realize a new restoration of our possibilities.

4. Laugh

"If you can laugh at it, you can live with it!"
— BRAD WILCOX

By far, one of the biggest obstacles we all face is taking life too seriously. We get so caught up trying to make our relationships work, finances balance, families function and businesses boom that we forget to look around and enjoy the ride we're on. I get it. I've been there. I know the pressures that bombard us each day can feel debilitating. We can find relief though, even if it is just for a moment.

"What did one eyeball say to the other eyeball?"

"I don't know what it is, but something between us smells."

The ability to smile and laugh allows any mental or physical struggle you face to temporarily disappear. I know that was a corny joke, but at the very least it made you smile, just a little bit. That's all it takes. I believe it's impossible to be anxious, angry, or sad when you're laughing. Our minds need to be let out on recess every now and then to climb the jungle gym, skip rope and forget about our daily worries and fears. So it's time to put more laughter in your life. Even if you have to open up your calendar, schedule it and set the alarm to remind you. A simple smile lights the fuse that leads to laughter, and laughter always explodes with a smile.

If the problem is that we don't have enough humor, how do we fix that? We need to search for that elusive smile or giggle and make it a priority. This may sound ridiculous, but as you're sitting in your cubicle at work, or driving your car to the grocery store, practice smiling. It will feel weird at first and you'll want to stop. Keep trying, though, and pretty soon an actual grin will take over. Whether this activity helps you start to feel better, or you laugh because of the looks you're getting from other cars driving by, it doesn't matter. At least for a moment you forgot your worries. Remember, it's hard to feel anxious, angry, or sad when laughing.

I'm convinced making light of a situation will not solve it, but can help you through it.

I think there is a place for sarcasm, but as my wife constantly reminds me, it's not very often. I still get dirty looks across the room from her because of a sarcastic comment I just made.

Four months after being paralyzed, my wife taught me the principle of laughing and humor in a way I will never forget. I was living at home again and it had been a long day of therapies, doctors and tremendous pain, so I was ready to go to sleep. My wife was putting some clothes away in our room as I sat in my wheelchair next to the bed. I looked over at my wife and impatiently said, "Could you hurry up? I need to lay down now." (I know, smooth move, huh?)

In a very nice way she walked up next to me, put me in a tight headlock and told me to apologize. Keep in mind I just broke my neck four months ago. Not to be outdone, I quickly flung my arm up around her neck and said, "Not till you let go first." We both smiled as we were squeezing and yelling. "Apologize!" "You let go first!" "Not till you apologize." Then I tightened my grip just a little more when boom! Her limp body collapsed across my legs and onto the carpet in front of me. She didn't move at all. I was stunned.

"Honey — are you okay?" I cautiously rolled forward and gently bumped her with the front of my wheelchair to see if she would move. "Time to get up, I need to get in bed." Nothing. I looked at her ribs to see if she was breathing. "You got me, joke's over." Then it hit me, I made my wife pass out and she could be hurt. What was I going to do? The phone was on the other side of the room and her body was blocking my path. She needs me! She needs my help and I feel trapped. I was scared for two reasons. First, she was hurt. Secondly, she was going to hurt me when she woke up.

After a few minutes, she slowly opened her eyes and delicately crawled onto the edge of the bed. "Uhhh. Are you okay? You passed out and fell to the floor." (I have *no* idea how that could have happened.) As I reached out to touch her shoulder, she sprang to her feet and yelled, pointing her finger at me, "Gotcha! You should have apologized!" She faked the whole thing!

Laughter is contagious and people are attracted to it. If you hear people laughing at the office, then go check it out. Invite one of your funnier friends over to your house and watch a movie you grew up laughing at. One of the most amazing attributes of laughter is it helps you forget judgment, fear and doubts. It is also very powerful in helping you forgive.

Smiling and laughter has to be part of your life, your trials and your healing. In good times and bad, smile!

5. Touch

"A touch can be to give life." —MICHELANGELO

The doctor pulls out a long thick needle and prepares to insert it straight into my abdomen to get a fluid sample from my stomach. Because of my paralysis, I won't be able to feel pain as the needle punctures my skin, but the muscles and organs just under that thin layer are fair game. I've never seen a needle that large, and I'm afraid the pain will be similar to a muscular man swinging an 8-pound sledgehammer on the top of a steel pole straight through me. My eyes begin to squint and I clench my teeth in preparation for what's about to occur, when out of nowhere I immediately start to relax. What just happened? I instantly feel that no matter how painful this gets, I will be okay.

I glance down and noticed my sweet wife tightly grasping my hand as if she wanted to take some of the pain away from me.

Touching someone you love actually reduces pain. When we don't feel loved and accepted from others, it is painful. Not disappointing, but actual "pain." If you have experienced this before, you know it can hurt as much as a broken bone.

Holding hands with someone can help comfort you and your brain through painful situations. A gentle pat on the shoulder, a soft touch of the arm or even legs beside each other while sitting on an airplane can be soothing and signal safety and trust. A hug that lasts at least three seconds or more can provide an enormous amount of fulfillment and confidence. These everyday gestures are usually taken for granted. Without any of this physical contact, you become touch-deprived. I have felt this for years and still suffer certain aspects of it today.

Sitting in a wheelchair all day makes it very awkward for others to provide me with the physical touch I yearn for. I'm not standing at the same level as everyone else — putting me outside of their comfort zones — so I'm not as easily noticed. It takes extra effort to bend over and hug me because it's so inconvenient. Most people don't know what to say or how to act when confronted by an individual with some form of a disability. Especially if it's really obvious, like a missing limb or wheelchair bound. I used to do this to before I broke my neck. Now I think it's funny as I watch people stare at me, but as I come closer they get very uncomfortable and start to ignore me.

I'm unable to sneak up behind my wife and give her a warm embrace when she's cooking in the kitchen. I can't throw my son on the couch and wrestle around the family room, trying to solidify my dominance in the house. It's even worse in public because most people don't know what to say to me, let alone put their hand on me. Many times the only real contact I feel in a day is when someone is helping me transfer into a vehicle or onto some furniture. Even then, I'm mostly paralyzed and can't feel a great deal of that. There are days that I long for the touch we all require.

Be the first to shake someone's hand and never turn down a hug, even if it is from your 90-year-old grandpa who tries to give you a peck on the lips as well. It will most likely be uncomfortable the first few times, but don't be afraid to ask others for a hug. Try not to be awkward, just be genuine.

Aside from everyone around you, there is another way to start filling your empty emotional cup: Go get a massage. To some this may sound crazy but to others it sounds like a heaven-sent idea. Massage therapy doesn't just help your muscles but it's great for your entire physical and mental being. This won't work for everyone, but studies have shown it can help with pain, fatigue, depression and improve your sleep. After a massage, I always feel more relaxed and focused.

Science is filled with studies showing how critical it is that we connect with other people on a physical level. The ability to touch, and be touched, is one of the greatest forms of communication we can use.

6. Therapy

"If you have a problem talk to a therapist, not Facebook."
—UNKNOWN

After a few years of me failing at wanting to progress, to truly accomplish anything significant, my wife came to me with a proposition. In reality, it was more like she told me what was going to happen. As a couple we were going to see a couples' therapist.

"Why do I need to see a therapist?" I thought.

"If you want to go I will support you, but not me."

This was embarrassing to even think about going, let alone actually showing up.

"Not me. I am normal and normal people don't go to therapists. What would my friends say if they found out?"

Our marriage was in need of some serious help, so I agreed to go knowing it would make Heather happier. That was my attitude, though. It was all about

Heather getting better and me helping her. This is how many people, in particular men, feel about any type of therapist, including sports therapy.

It hurts our ego to admit we are not strong enough physically or mentally to handle it ourselves. Women, on the other hand, are much smarter than us and quicker to admit a problem. Their excuses, however, are usually along the lines of being way too busy to spend the time and money on themselves when there are so many others that need their help first.

Once you've applied a few different techniques to remedy the situation that has you feeling *frozen*, and you're still struggling, it may be time to get professional help. There is no need to feel embarrassed in getting some counseling.

I'll admit it — I felt like a failure when I first went through the doors because I couldn't do it on my own. The guidance I received, though, gave me a greater understanding of how I think and helped create a plan of action that would work best for my wife and me. My therapist and I are good friends to this day.

Depression, anxiety and chronic pain are real! They have the ability to affect anyone and everyone. It doesn't matter your age, gender, skin color, religion, or favorite TV show. They're not politically correct and don't care whether you just went through a life-altering challenge last month.

The most incredible people I know have climbed out of the depths of suffering, defeat, terrible losses, and spiritual uncertainty. Because of their resilience, they now share with others the most genuine compassion, love and understanding I've ever seen. The rocky road you are traveling now is giving you the opportunity to reach great heights in the future.

CHAPTER QUESTIONS:

If my best friend came to me with the same problem, what would I tell them?

_____

_____

_____

What are three ways I will integrate more laughter and joy into my life?

_____

_____

_____

Which one of my friends could be depressed or dealing with anxiety and needs my help?

_____

_____

By what date will I contact them and in what way am
I of most service?

_____

_____

_____

_____

_____

5

You're Not The Only One Freezing

"A man may fall many times,
but he won't be a failure until he says
someone pushed him." —ELMER G. LETTERMAN

Is A HAPPY AND PRODUCTIVE LIFE based on you, others, or a combination of both? Many times we can be so focused on ourselves, and what we feel we deserve, that it can destroy us in the end. The following experience shared by a friend of mine (whom I'll call Katie) illustrates the dangers of the "it's-all-about-me" philosophy.

Katie was working in California at a highly sought-after company as an administrator. She was a very smart and accomplished businesswoman who was excited about this new opportunity. Katie was placed in a cluster of three other women who were also lead admins for their respective departments. A woman named Peggy was the top dog of administrators. She had worked at the business for more than 20 years and was revered by all department heads, with extra responsibilities and privileges. People trusted her and knew she had important institutional memory for past projects. She knew who could influence other top decision-makers, who would fight against certain planning projects and different tactics to sway the CEO. Peggy certainly sat in the golden chair.

As Katie began working there, she immediately learned her place. Without hesitation, she embraced Peggy and supported her. Stories were shared, family crises were covered and picnics were planned. This group of four administrators became quick friends and everything seemed to be running without a hitch. Peggy went about her regular routine: She would leave early, come late and take care of family issues during self-appointed three-hour lunches. No one seemed to take issue with it, so neither did Katie.

However, what Katie wasn't aware of was the fact that she was expected to "cover" for Peggy. Not just cover for her, but answer her phones, respond to emails, file documents, prepare papers and lie to Peggy's boss.

When Peggy's boss came calling, Katie would make countless excuses for her. But none of this was a secret. Peggy acted as if everyone knew about her behavior and it was expected, like she had earned it. She would talk about her work practices openly to the other office staff so my friend assumed everyone knew what she was doing, including upper management. Katie loved her job and those she worked with. Nothing was ever discussed with management, or anyone else, that wasn't true.

Over time the innocent comments by Katie started raising concern about Peggy's behavior. Her boss and entire department began questioning Peggy's behavior and checked up on her daily to ensure she was in the office and fulfilling her responsibilities, not delegating them to someone else. This deeply offended Peggy.

"Why would someone do this to me? I'm above this kind of treatment and haven't done anything wrong."

Over the next few months, the conveniences Peggy felt she deserved were being slowly stripped away. She took issue with Katie, continuously thinking she was out to destroy her. The confidence everyone once shared in Peggy was crumbling. Tensions were rising and a lack of loyalty began to prevail in the workplace and it strained once-close friendships. Stark glances were given and rude comments made toward Katie,

Peggy gave her notice she would be quitting.

After the office parties, gifts and farewell hugs, Peggy went to Katie and said, "This is all *your* fault! You did this to me!" Can you believe that? Unfortunately, this happens all the time. In Peggy's mind she felt it was all about *her*. Peggy lost sight that she was hired to do a certain job, and because of a job well done she earned privileges. Not a free pass.

Her short statement summed it up perfectly. "This is all your fault."

Peggy has her views, her wants, her expectations, and yes, even some privileges, but there's no way it could be her fault in her mind. She saw her position as an entitlement that took precedence over doing the job. Who was really the problem here?

Words and phrases often used by someone like this are: you, they, I didn't, and because. All of these redirect the center of attention to someone else or give excuses for their actions, making them look flawless. Rarely ever is responsibility accepted, unless it is positive. Is this the kind of friend you want to have? Do you know someone like this, or are you that person others have a hard time being around?

If this is you, my first instinct would be to slap you silly and kick you off the "it's-all-about-me" ledge. However, since I can't swing my arms fast or move my legs, let's try another route. Here are four tips to help keep us from only focusing on ourselves. I have to refer back to them regularly.

1. Put yourself in their shoes

Before you begin yelling at the nurse because it's taking so long for the doctor to come inspect your sick child, think about how she might be feeling. She could be tired from being on her feet for eight hours straight, overwhelmed from having to oversee so many patients at once, or just feeling frustrated about a family problem at home. Is it really necessary for you to make her feel terrible just to get what you want?

I've learned that if I'm more understanding and nice, then people are willing to help me in more ways than I asked. This is not a new concept. Since I rely so much on others to assist me each day, this thought process has become essential. When someone is physically lifting you into a tall van or airplane, it's comforting to know that they like you. Nobody wants to help someone who is rude and demanding.

It doesn't have to be someone's fault either. I have had young kids trip on my foot and fall down crying while walking around my wheelchair. I wouldn't apologize because I felt it wasn't my fault. I'm pretty sure I didn't move my foot so why should I apologize? I was so caught up in making sure I wasn't at fault that I couldn't even say I'm sorry to a 3-year-old with tears in her eyes. I should feel sorry that they were hurt and not worry about how I look.

2. Ask for what you need versus what you want

We can confuse the idea of needing something with the impression that we want something. Do you need to win the argument with your spouse or do you just want to? Would your life still be okay if you ate at

Chili's instead of Applebee's? I think it would. This is not always easy. I'm not saying you should never stand up for yourself and get what you desire. Just stop, step back, and decide if you really need it or just want it.

3. Use "we" more often

One of the most effective ways I've found to put many situations into perspective and diffuse any tension is to insert the word "we" into my comment. Instead of using you, your, or my, try saying *we*, even if you're not responsible. For example:

"We weren't able to make the final shot that lost the game for us. Next time we'll get it."

"There are mistakes in our report, maybe we could fix them?"

"Look at that. We put my shoes on the wrong feet. Let's try switching them." (My wife and caregivers have done this to me multiple times.)

I understand that last one only applies to me, but it works perfectly. By using words like we, our, let's and us, any hard feelings seem to dissipate. The general tone of the situation shifts the focus to finding solutions instead of attaching blame.

4. Practice putting yourself last

Don't be the person who always thinks me, me, me. Other people are just as special as you and they deserve to get their way sometimes. Make a goal of putting yourself last in at least one situation every day this week. That's not too much to ask. Next time you're doing something, whether you're waiting in line to dish your food at dinner, or picking your seat on the city bus, wait and let other people choose what they like first. Don't think that you somehow deserve more than others just because you are "you."

If you want to take it a step further then select one person, and for the next week make them the No. 1 priority in your life. Put their needs before yours and see just how amazing you feel seven days later. If you choose to take on this challenge, what is the name of the incredible individual you can selflessly serve for a week?

I will put _____'s needs first for the next week.

This next story emphasizes aspects of selfishness I didn't know I possessed.

On an early fall evening my wife and I were driving home from a date night with two other couples who are close friends of ours. It was an enjoyable time doing service for others, topping the night off with some frozen yogurt and laughter. We all left our separate ways with me behind the wheel of our big Ford truck. We were eager to see if our kids had accomplished the only two tasks we asked: clean up the dishes from dinner and everyone asleep by 10:30. Anyone with children knows that anything over one request is usually lost in translation, but we had high hopes.

I glanced over to see Heather in a stunning new dress with a big smile on her face as she looked back at me. I couldn't be more honored to wear the gold ring she gave me, symbolizing the love I have for this beautiful woman. On the inside of the ring she had engraved two simple words, "Eternally Yours." I owed this amazing woman more than I could ever repay.

Her life had been flipped upside down two separate times in just 13 months with my neck breaks. She's now being forced to live with the harsh consequences of someone else's poor choices. Heather had almost every reason to walk away into a different life with less anxiety and fear. She chose to stay with me, though, and I am eternally grateful.

Off to my left the bright lights of a vehicle caught my attention as it was rapidly driving toward the stop sign at the end of its neighborhood. I cautiously watched as our paths came closer. They began to slow down so my focus went back to the road ahead of me.

The next thing I know a large SUV is rocketing across the lane next to me, aimed directly at my driver side door. I quickly swerved to my right trying to avoid a collision as Heather screamed, "Look out!" The powerful impact from the front of their car knocked my hands off the brake pedal and steering wheel, throwing my body across the middle console. Thank heavens for seatbelts or my head may have slammed into Heather.

My truck changed directions and veered toward a different neighborhood as I scrambled to sit up and get control of the vehicle. I felt so vulnerable, like everything was in slow motion and I'm reaching for anything to grab onto and stop what was about to happen. I couldn't reach the hand control that applies the brakes, putting an end to all this. Heather yelled once more as we smashed head-on into a large boulder pushing it aside. We then slammed into a heavy cement culvert, lifting it's tremendous weight halfway out of the ground. We stopped just a few yards short of punching a hole through the side of someone's house.

The truck snapped both axles, destroyed the front end and had extensive body damage along the driver's side where the other vehicle struck us. Even though airbags didn't deploy, that Ford truck saved our lives. Other than a little shaken up, I felt pretty good. I looked over to see how Heather was. Her forehead was bleeding from being hurled into the front dash with her glasses on. She was complaining of some head pain but couldn't clearly define any other injuries.

The EMTs looked Heather over, put a bandage on her forehead, but didn't take either of us to the hospital. They weren't too concerned and felt we would be fine. I wanted to go home but Heather had other plans. I quickly called our friends and they circled back to pick us up and go to the ER for a second opinion. X-rays looked clear, and though Heather's head and neck still hurt, we were released. Probably just whiplash and a minor abrasion on the forehead. With rest and time it will get better, we were told.

The lady who used her vehicle as a bullet that night, was charged with her third DUI and wasn't injured at all. Go figure.

The next two weeks were especially difficult in our family as both parents suffered from severe whiplash and other minor scrapes, but I healed more quickly than Heather. This wasn't what we were used to. Usually I was the one with setbacks and injuries. Heather's muscles were tight. She suffered daily migraines and was nauseous and lethargic.

"That's okay, I can take care of her and the family till she gets better," I thought. "This will only last for a few days because I'm the quadriplegic, and the car slammed into *my* door, not hers. If I wasn't hurt that bad then she will recover quickly. She's a very strong person."

At first it wasn't too bad as we all jumped in to help anywhere we could. All right, I didn't jump anywhere, but I would have. Getting up extra early to get kids off to school, taking care of meals, making sure laundry was done, shopping, assisting with homework, and a thousand more tasks. All while creating a business and trying to take care of Heather. I did have tons of help from family and friends, but most of all, it was our four amazing children. They were extraordinary in the service and sacrifice they gave to support their mom. She means everything to them.

Heather was completely out of commission as she slept in a recliner almost 18 hours a day and complained of relentless migraines, harsh muscle spasms and nausea. I didn't know why she wasn't getting better, and many of the pain killers only made her more drowsy. My wife was suffering in a way I had never seen before. When I tried to communicate with her, she was very forgetful and troubled. The doctors said she probably had a minor concussion but will recover shortly. "That sounds doable — we've overcome worse than this."

As the days went on and her health didn't improve, I became frustrated. I'm giving, and giving, and giving — how long could I sustain this? "It has to end soon," I thought, "because I need some attention pointing back in my direction."

Can you believe what I started doing? Doesn't that sound ridiculously selfish? My wife is drowning and I'm thinking more of my well-being than hers. For years now I'm the one who had most of the attention and our lives really revolved around me. Now that our situation had flipped, I was showing just how weak I really was.

It had been almost two months since the accident and no one seemed to know what was really wrong with my wife. I couldn't take it anymore and decided the best remedy was for her to push herself harder and for her to start doing more around the house. This much sacrifice was unfair to me and had gone on long enough. I needed some help. Maybe this would be what she needed to snap out of this.

So I wouldn't fix certain meals, clean up all the dirty laundry, have the dishwasher emptied, and other chores she usually did. I would then ask Heather to please get them done and put pressure on her to start taking care of the family again. I wasn't mean and I never yelled, but I'm sure the guilt I placed on her was almost unbearable.

My thoughts turned toward myself. "I've felt similar pain and anxiety and you must punch through it." "You've got to get up, your kids are asking for their mother again. They need you." "It's been a long time and I need some affection. Where did my wife go?"

Weeks continued to pass with Heather showing very little improvement. All this turmoil and uncertainty was taking a harsh toll on her physically and mentally. She knew the doctors had misdiagnosed her injuries but no one would believe her. Her body weight had diminished to a fragile 95 pounds and a very close friend even accused her of becoming addicted to pain medications. She needed answers and support. My job as a loving husband is not just to believe *in* her, but to *believe* her. She must have felt hopelessly alone.

I even entertained the thought that Heather was exaggerating her symptoms and dragging this whole scenario out longer than it needed to be. I was pressuring and manipulating my best friend so I could get what I wanted. I even made her drive to the school and pick up our little girls because I was tired of doing it. That was a lot of extra work for me to get in and out of my truck for such a short drive. It was unsafe for Heather to drive alone because of her poor depth perception and an unbalanced equilibrium, but I insisted anyway. I put my wife and children's lives at risk because I was too lazy to get up and do it.

Shortly after this Heather was finally re-diagnosed. The doctors told her she had suffered a brain trauma from the accident that had partially injured her brain and severely tore muscles in her back. This caused impaired memory, extreme fatigue, unbearable migraines and excruciating muscle pain. She was right all along. She usually is.

After months of mental exercises, rest and physical therapies, Heather recovered tremendously. However, she still suffers from tight muscles in her neck and minor memory loss at times.

Throughout this ordeal I learned that I am no better than anyone else when it comes to being selfish and just thinking about me. By shifting the focus to myself, I'm convinced I severely crippled Heather's healing process. She lost a great deal of trust in me because I tripped and fell trying to stand by her side. It has taken me years to regain the faith Heather lost in me during this difficult time in our life. I lived each day more fixated on what I felt I deserved, than making sacrifices for the ones I love.

At first I did my best trying to put myself last and take care of my family. I even successfully put Heather's needs above my own for a period of time, but I failed to put myself in her shoes. As much as anyone, I know exactly what it's like to feel alone and trapped — that no one understands what you're going through. Why couldn't I have taken that knowledge and applied it more effectively to this situation? Why couldn't I have held on a little longer and demonstrated a more infinite faith and love for my wife?

You're not perfect and you never will be. Neither will I. Every situation changes, but one thing will always stay the same — our ability to choose. You can choose not to play your trump card. You can choose to put others first. You can choose to be happy and successful. Nobody owes you anything and you're not entitled to greatness, you must earn it one good act at a time. The most extraordinary people in life are those who build up everyone around them.

The sooner we can recognize the power we hold to create magnificent change in our lives, we will feel empowered to achieve our greatest desires. Let's go make an incredible difference!

CHAPTER QUESTIONS:

When was the last time I chose to be happy rather than demanding to be right?

_____

_____

_____

_____

_____

In what ways can I put others first this week?

_____

_____

_____

_____

_____

What inspiring qualities do others possess that I would like to possess?

_____

_____

_____

_____

_____

_____

How can I implement those traits into my life?

_____

_____

_____

_____

_____

_____

_____

6

~~~~~~~~~~~~~~~~~~~~~~~~~~~~~~~

A Drop Of Understanding

"The most basic of all human needs is the need to understand and be understood. The best way to understand people is to listen to them." —RALPH NICHOLS

WHEN WE'RE TALKING ABOUT OVERCOMING TRIALS and facing fears, the more people I talk with, the more I find that we all just want to be understood. Everyone wants what they say and feel to be important.

Exactly 22 days after breaking my neck the first time, I was flown on a small two prop medical plane from Bend, Oregon, to my hometown of Boise, Idaho. Then transported by ambulance to the Elks Rehabilitation Hospital in downtown Boise. This was one of the best facilities throughout the northwest for my recovery. Over the next three weeks I made miraculous improvements, but I was still far from being able to run with my kids again.

Shortly after my arrival, the recreational therapist introduced my wife and I to another couple just a few doors down. When I was pushed by wheelchair into the other patient's room, the first thing I noticed was the man was missing one-third of his skull. The skin still covered Scott's head but the bone no longer protected his brain. It was hard speaking to him without looking at this terrible injury. Scott's beautiful wife sat lovingly by his side and briefly shared with us their story.

They had only been married a couple of years and were excited about their new life together, hoping to start a family soon. While living in eastern Idaho, he was involved in a major car accident crushing parts of his body. Scott's devoted wife did most of the speaking and it quickly became evident why. It was difficult for Scott to form a complete sentence, making it challenging to communicate with others. Most of his words came out sounding wrong and he had a labored stutter.

As we spent more time with this couple I began feeling an emotion I didn't want, but couldn't avoid. Jealousy. I was jealous that Scott could walk down the hallway, stand up and give his wife a big hug, pick up an M&M with his fingers, go to the bathroom on his own, and much, much more. He could do all these activities that I badly wanted to. This made me feel like I was so far behind and would never catch up.

A couple weeks later our therapist took both of us and our wives bowling. Though not perfect, Scott could slowly carry the heavy black ball in his hand and roll it down the smooth lane towards the pins. I could barely pick up a pencil with two hands.

"Scott was so lucky! I wanted what he had. Even with his weaknesses his life must still be better than mine," I thought.

"Nothing is more validating and affirming than being understood."
—STEPHEN R. COVEY

During the next 10 frames, my jealousy turned to sympathy as I watched him struggle to form sentences of excitement over how many pins were knocked down. He would also abruptly lash out at his wife and others for no reason. Scott's faithful wife explained to us that because of the brain injury, he is loving and kind one minute and yelling and swearing the next. Scott was never like this before his accident and he doesn't know that he's even doing this to her. I'm sure if he knew, he would be mortified.

You can see in his eyes that he understands and comprehends what you've said, and is trying to give the correct response, but his comments are unrelated to the topic. How unbelievably frustrating that must feel to try and say or do one thing, and have it come out completely different. Over the next few weeks as we got to know them better, my testimony of one important principle became very clear: I'll take my problems.

That day bowling I promised myself to never judge others. We don't understand everyone's situation, and probably never will. It could be much worse than our own, and usually is. If my body had landed ½ inch in any different direction while skiing, I could be like Scott. I lost the ability to function in many various ways that make my life physically and mentally difficult. What was taken from Scott, though, was his personality, his identity, ultimately himself.

Which situation would you rather have?

I would much rather lose the use of my limbs than lose the use of my mind. What an endless hell that must be for Scott. I get frustrated just thinking about it. The perception of his wants and needs are clear, but they can't be realized by others due to a lack of understanding and communication. How do you choose to fight and be victorious when you can't fully comprehend — and constantly keep forgetting — what choices you've already made?

For most of us, our situations will never be as serious as Scott's, but we can still feel extremely helpless and like no one gets it or can relate to us. The biggest reason we want to feel understood is the need for approval and validation. What I'm going through is real, I'm not faking it! We want to sense that others aren't blaming us for what we're experiencing, that they've accepted our situation, and are willing to help. How is this accomplished though?

The following four tips have helped me feel more understood and even helped me to better understand others.

1. Be patient

It can be frustrating that others just don't get it the way I do. They think differently and have different life experiences to draw from. We're not meant to be the same, and that's what makes life so exciting. Those close to you really do care and want to relate to your situation, but many times are incapable of doing so. Don't be too hard on them — they really are trying. Just be patient.

2. Talk positively

Whether or not we realize it, we are constantly talking to ourselves, saying how well we did at one thing and not as good at another. What we say every day truly impacts the way we feel and how we act.

Tell yourself, "I'm doing okay right now and I am capable of completing hard things. I'm strong and I will get through this. I will not be affected by the negative opinions of others."

Pay close attention to the last part. Someone else's opinion has nothing to do with you. You have an exclusive right to create your own thoughts and feelings, no one else.

3. Keep looking

Never stop searching for someone who can relate to your worries, emotions and pain. There are others who have felt very similar hopes and fears. I say similar because no one knows exactly how you feel, so don't expect that from them. Only twice in the last 14 years have I run into another person that is dealing with similar physical pain and paralysis. Usually it's one or the other. What a rush of relief it is to speak with someone who shares the same highs and lows. It's hard to describe the comfort I felt when speaking with these individuals because they *truly* understood my situation. I didn't have to explain all of the frustrations and conflict I live with. They got it. This gives me the hope to keep pushing forward knowing that they are striving to progress as well. I'm not alone.

4. Find your purpose

By finding what you live for, what makes you tick, what gives you the energy to live life each day, you'll be able to round up the inner desire needed to push forward. In the next chapter we will discuss in greater detail the topic of finding your purpose and passion.

The following personal story illustrates my desperate need to be understood. I rarely ever talk about this in detail because it affects me so deeply: the tremendous physical pain I feel on an hourly basis. I don't share this much with others for a few different reasons. The first is more of a prideful reason, I guess. I want to be the strong husband and father who doesn't complain about his problems. I don't want others to look at me and feel sorry all the time, especially my family. I don't need the pity.

Secondly, I'm hesitant to discuss my pain much with others because I don't think it does any good. Most people can't relate to the constant battle I'm engaged in, so I don't open up about it.

On a pain scale of 1 to 10, (10 being the worst) the severe stinging and burning I feel everywhere I'm paralyzed never dips below a 5, and often reaches an 8 or 9. The best way I can describe this is like sitting on an open fireplace, burning. We've tried all kinds of remedies and medications but the doctors can't control it. For the first two years this intense fire scorching my body never dropped below a 7. This was excruciating and it required every ounce of energy to fight the torment. This extraordinary sensation had seized a large portion of my focus, paralyzing me mentally from being present with my surroundings and responsibilities. If I didn't find relief soon they would have to put me in an insane asylum. I'm joking about that last part, kind of.

Once we found some medication that finally helped balance me around a level 5, a different type of pain began in my abdomen. It felt like I was being stabbed by small double edged knives throughout my stomach, bladder and other internal organs and muscles. This lasted all day long but would extremely heighten towards the evening and throughout the night. It was hard enough fighting a battle of burning nerve pain, but now I was being attacked on two fronts. This lasted for almost a year and brought me to my "metaphoric" knees. The doctors acted like they knew how I felt, but in reality, no one seemed to understand what I was going through. I was searching for the reassurance it would be okay.

I couldn't find it.

I vividly remember Heather and I attending a friend's Hawaiian luau six months after breaking my neck. While sitting in my wheelchair on their back patio, everyone was asking questions and wanting to talk to me. All I could think about was how the bones in my right ankle felt like they were being slowly crushed between two large boulders. This was on top of the burning throughout my body. It was miserable and we couldn't get it to stop. I desperately wanted relief from this terrible agony. Maybe I should go home and try to sleep, because when I'm sleeping that's the only time I don't feel pain. But there is no way I could fall asleep hurting like this. I tried to explain to some close buddies what it felt like but all I got were blank stares and words of disbelief.

"But you're paralyzed, you can't feel anything." I was told.

Some medical professionals tried to explain that it was all in my head. It's probably just messages being sent from your brain to your body that are being mis-directed where you broke your neck. They should go away eventually. At that point it didn't matter whether it was real or not, I just knew that no one was under-standing the never-ending anguish I was experiencing. I had to tell myself that we will find an answer, the pain will go away, this is all for a greater purpose and I can handle it.

I'm fully aware that no one present at that party could take away the pain, so I tried to be patient. They all loved me and supported me but were incapable of helping me. However, I truly believe if anyone could have even remotely empathized with my suffering, I would surely have found some relief. Being paralyzed physically is devastating, but the mental battles can be far worse.

I was constantly afraid others were thinking the pain wasn't that bad and I was just imagining some of it. Or that I was looking for attention and milking the situation of my paralysis as long as I could. I just wanted someone who could understand, even a little bit.

If you're not able to put yourself in their shoes then try these following ideas. When done properly, they've made me more willing to open up and allow others in.

1. Listen intently

When someone listens intently to you, it makes you feel accepted, understood, important and validated. You are reminded that you're not invisible or alone. Being an effective listener can be difficult, that's why there aren't many out there. Also, don't be too quick to react, provide solutions or disagree. Most of all, try not to be judgmental. Remember, it's all about the other person.

~~~~~~~

"Most people don't listen with the intent to understand; they listen with intent to reply."
—STEPHEN R. COVEY

~~~~~~~

2. Ask genuinely

Ask thoughtful questions to get a better under-standing. If you don't really care about the answer, then don't ask it. Ask open-ended questions that allow them to share their feelings, not just facts. Such as, "How does this affect..." or "tell me about..."

3. Pick your words wisely

Even if you can relate to their situation, be very careful how you communicate that to them. Try to stay away from words like "I know," "I understand," "I get it," or "you don't," and "you should." Any of these words combined in your sentence can be an instant turn off and may offend the person you're trying to help.

As you search to be understood, remember that it's a two-way street. Be willing to open up and communicate with those you trust, your deepest worries and pain, along with your greatest highs and happiness. Even if they can't relate to you, give them a chance to try. I've suppressed some of these emotions for 14 years and am now just beginning to share them. I wish I would have done this long ago.

CHAPTER QUESTIONS

In what ways do I feel misunderstood?

_____

_____

_____

_____

_____

_____

What more will I do to experience the peace of acceptance of being understood?

_____

_____

_____

_____

_____

What can others do to better understand my needs?

_____

_____

_____

_____

_____

_____

I will share these ideas with them by what date?

_____

_____

_____

_____

_____

_____

_____

_____

7

~~~~~~~~~~~~~~~~~~~~~~~~~~~~~~~~

Flowing Into Your Purpose

"If you can't figure out your purpose, figure out your passion. For your passion will lead you right into your purpose." — BISHOP T.D. JAKES

DESPITE ALL THE DIFFERENCES that separate our cultures and beliefs in this world, we share one common thread that can't be escaped: We all have trials. In different ways and at different levels, but in the end it's a battle we must fight in order to survive. There is a tremendous purpose found through struggling. It seems to weed out all the fluff that is blinding us from seeing our true vision. It is what transforms us into the person we are and molds us into the people we will become.

What is your purpose? What gets you through the day? What is your passion or highest vision for life? Most people are walking around aimlessly not knowing what they really want. They go to work or school, fulfill their role in their family, maybe even get involved in their church or community, but never really push themselves to achieve more. You can live your whole life feeling like you have contributed and been successful in many ways, while still never knowing what your purpose has been or should be.

Think for a moment. What really makes you happy and gives you purpose?

My life seemed perfect with my career, my family, my faith and my home. Sure we wanted more, but everything was on track and moving in the right direction. I was happy. I thought my purpose was to just keep moving forward. I only saw the big picture and never focused too much on the details. Then I broke my neck and almost died before I realized what I was really living for.

Now I know.

A few days after being pulled off the ski hill, I slowly opened my eyes to find myself lying on a bed in the ICU of a hospital. I tried to sit up and figure out what was going on, but my body remained motionless. The intense pain I originally experienced on the ski hill was now all throughout my body and it was torturous.

The door opened and my wife came over to my bed-side with a big smile and told me she loved me. The pain I was feeling momentarily left as I knew my best friend was by my side. I knew we could accomplish anything together. I quickly said, "I love you," back, but nothing came out of my mouth. Why couldn't I talk? What was going on? What did I look like? She cautiously picked up a small mirror and held it high above my bed.

What I saw was hard to comprehend and even harder to describe. I was completely paralyzed throughout my whole body and battling a fierce temperature of 104° for days that the doctors couldn't control. There was a long feeding tube that traveled up through my right nostril and down to my stomach. Fourteen different wires, monitors, tubes and injection sites were stuck into more parts of my body than I realized I had. A metal halo (not a shiny gold one) was literally screwed into my skull in four places to help give stability for my neck to heal properly. The worst of all, though, was a tracheostomy was performed on my throat attaching a ventilator to breathe for me — my lungs and diaphragm were too weak by themselves. Due to this procedure, I was unable to speak or easily communicate with anyone.

I couldn't talk to my wife and let her know it was going to be okay, that we would get through this. The only physical power I still possessed was to blink my eyelids. I went from being able to climb mountains, swim across rivers, and challenge the impossible, to lying on a bed motionless, powerless and helpless. What was I going to do to get out of this situation? I needed a plan. But how do you set goals and plan for the future when you're not sure there is one?

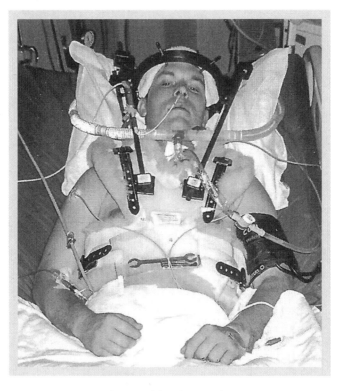

My snow skiing neck break December 22, 2001

I desperately wanted to see my young children but they weren't allowed in my room. Maybe that was for the best — it could be devastating having them see me like this. Just when I thought it couldn't get any worse, my nurse briskly walked into the room and introduced herself as Helga. Are you kidding me? Helga sounded like the villain in a James Bond movie. The one with a big scar on their face who's brought in to inflict pain and extract sensitive information. "I'm willing to talk, what do you want to know?"

Heather had gone home for the night and the nurses left me alone to try and get some sleep. While staring at the clock on the wall and attempting to comprehend the life-altering events in my life, the ventilator breathing for me started to malfunction. There was a *long* space in between each breath I received and it continued to get farther ... and farther .... apart. "It's okay, I'm sure there is an alarm going off at the nurses station and someone will be right in to fix it," I thought. No alarms went off and no one came in to check on me.

I was running out of air! I frantically tried to move my arms and legs to hit a button, pull out of wire, or make some type of noise. I even opened my mouth and screamed for help. But my body was still and my voice was silent.

I was frozen.

I was suffocating in the most-watched area of the hospital and there's nothing I can do about it. So I did the only thing I knew I could do.

I peacefully closed my eyes, pictured myself kneeling down next to the bed and said a prayer.

I began to relax and focus on the only thing I could control — my mind. As I prayed my thoughts were flooded with many conflicting emotions. Was this my time to go? If all I could do was lay in bed the rest of my life and have others take care of me, I didn't want that. Maybe my kids would be better off with a dad that could pick them up and chase them around the park. Will Heather be okay? She needs a husband who can stand by her and hold her in joyful and troubling times. I don't know if I'll ever be able to do this again. They didn't sign up for this. Maybe it will be easier on everyone if this machine quits working altogether. These are very difficult and scary thoughts. Is it really worth the difficult fight this would be?

As the ventilator was giving me what I thought was one of my very last breaths, the answer swelled up inside me. Yes! I *do* want to live, and it *is* worth fighting for!

I want to see my daughter in white and dance with her at her wedding. I can't wait to run around the backyard teaching my son how to throw a football. I deserve to be the man who's firmly holding my wife's hand while walking along the beach at sunset. I should be the one who's cutting down a large Griswold tree with my family, and opening presents Christmas morning. I will do what it takes to be there for them.

Just then the nurse walked in the room and I thought, "My prayers have been answered." I was out of oxygen and options. Helga picked up my chart, wrote down a few numbers and looked down at me. I began blinking like a crazy man because, well, that's all I could do. If I knew Morse code I would've tried to communicate that way with my eyelids. She put the chart down, gradually turned around and began to leave the room.

"Wait! Stop! This can't be happening. I just decided to live!" I screamed in my head.

Then I did something I've never done before. I began to softly click my tongue on the roof of my mouth. Click, click, click. My mouth was so dry you could barely hear it. She heard it though, slowly turned around, and began walking over next to the side of my bed staring at me. I did it again. Click, click, click. She looked at my chest for a moment and then quickly back to the machines. I could see the fear in her eyes as she immediately reached over to the ventilator and adjusted its gauges. Whooooooh! Talk about a breath of fresh air.

While the oxygen slowly filled my empty lungs again I felt a tremendous sigh of relief, but it was much more than that. My deflated aspirations and dreams were now overflowing with life's most powerful medicine. Hope. My prayers were answered. I was going to live. I would be there for my wife and kids!

Having a near-death experience like that really helped me find my purpose. It wasn't my career, house, or anything else. It was my wife and kids. Now I knew where to put all my energy and focus.

When you find your purpose that doesn't mean it will never change. It will shift throughout your life depending upon what is relevant at the time as we evolve physically, emotionally and spiritually. During that moment, my goal was to get as healthy as possible so I could be there for my family. They were my purpose. Today that has expanded to include assisting others in living an *unfrozen* life. I want to help others attain happiness and success by making and acting upon correct choices. This is what I feel I'm supposed to do and where I can make the greatest impact.

We need to continually re-evaluate why we do what we do. Life will change and your purpose must adapt with it.

When people ask, "What is my life purpose?" what they're actually asking is, "What can I do with my time that is important and fulfilling?" We have to start somewhere. As we progress forward, our vision will become clearer and we will find the happiness we desire. The following four concepts may help you find your purpose:

1. Past pain

"In our deepest pain, lies our highest purpose." It doesn't mean our life purpose has to come from pain, but it's a good place to start looking. Doing hard things deepens and strengthens the body, mind and spirit. What's been your most painful challenge in life? What did you focus on that helped you get through it?

2. Through your passion

We've all had that experience where we get so wrapped up in something that minutes turned into hours and hours turn into, "Oh, man, I forgot to eat." What was it that made you do that? Don't just look at the activity you were doing but look at the principles behind those activities. It may not be playing video games that you love, but your passion for improvement and getting better at something. It's the competition with others and yourself that really drives you. Now, how can you apply those principles to other aspects of your life?

3. Spiritually and emotionally

If you are religious and feel you have a relationship with your Maker, then you can relate to this. Right now, there is something you feel you should do — something you think about doing — yet you don't do it. Through prayer you may be searching to find out what your mission is here on this Earth. What are those impressions, and what are the reasons you haven't acted on them? What we truly care about usually scares us the most.

〜〜〜〜〜

"Ask, and it shall be given you; seek, and ye shall find; knock, and it shall be opened unto you." —MATTHEW 7:7

〜〜〜〜〜

The divine guidance you're being given is prompting you toward that purpose. I feel this, and you might, too. Don't be afraid of others' opinions. Don't worry about whether or not you're capable of fulfilling this responsibility. If you know exactly how to do it, you're not dreaming big enough. You are talented, gifted and have tremendous possibilities.

4. Ask others

It might be time to ask others for help. It can be difficult to see where you truly shine because you're too close, and possibly critical of yourself. Your friends, family members and professionals (such as coworkers and coaches) have a different view and perspective than you. They may be able to share different ambitions and talents you possess, that point you in a direction you were meant to go.

A worthwhile purpose consists of one main principle: Are you willing to suffer and sacrifice to see it completed? If you truly have found what puts a smile on your face and gives you a sense of inner peace, then you will need to fight for it.

"Passion is the *result of action*, not the cause of it." You can't sit idly by waiting for everything to happen for you. Go make it happen! Go struggle for what you believe in! Go experience fulfillment and happiness! Go live a life you will not regret! Go live your purpose and passion!

CHAPTER QUESTIONS:

What really makes me happy and gives me purpose?

_____

_____

_____

_____

_____

How can I inject more of this in my life?

_____

_____

_____

_____

_____

During my most difficult challenges what do I focus
on that helps me get through them?

_____

_____

_____

_____

_____

_____

_____

How have I been able to help others because of the
adversity I've faced?

_____

_____

_____

_____

_____

8

Who's In Your Raft?

"If you want to go fast, go alone.
If you want to go far, go together."
—AFRICAN PROVERB

WHO'S ON YOUR SIDE OF THE BATTLEFIELD when the first shot has been fired and bullets are whizzing past your head? When you're wounded, hurting and scared, do you have someone willing to run into danger and carry you to protection? More importantly, are you the kind of person who runs into uncertainty, to give the lifesaving hope needed by so many others? I fully believe the amount of support we receive from others is vital to our personal success, which then allows us to more effectively serve others.

What is a support system? The medical definition is a network of people who provide an individual with practical or emotional support. I believe it's much deeper than that. This special group of individuals should know you, care for you, and be willing to sacrifice their own wants for your success and happiness. They love you.

How does a superior support system help?

- ❖ A powerful sense of belonging
- ❖ Accountability
- ❖ More self-confidence
- ❖ Better problem solving
- ❖ Greater peace of mind
- ❖ Improved health

While living in Utah for intense therapy, I received a phone call from a friend who asked if I would do them a favor. They wondered if Heather and I would go down to a local hospital and visit a friend of theirs that had recently been injured. We'll call her Sarah. We had seen a number of individuals before so I promptly asked what the situation was.

Sarah had been in a terrible auto accident two weeks earlier. Her young teenage son, who had just passed his driver's test, drove through a stop sign in their Honda Accord with Sarah in the passenger seat. A large semi- truck slammed into the side of their car, crushing their vehicle like a tin can. The EMTs treated her son for some minor injuries while Sarah was taken by helicopter to the hospital with life-threatening complications. She severely damaged her spinal cord leaving her nearly completely paralyzed.

Fourteen days passed and she was still in the ICU receiving critical care when I was asked to help. I told them I'm not sure what I could do at this point but we would be more than happy to try.

Sarah was 50 years old and lived in a small country town in central Utah. Her husband provided for the family as a farmer while she taught part time at the local school. The two had been blessed with wonderful children who learned by example the value of hard work. Putting money in the savings account each month rarely happened, but they always had clothes and food. A few of the children had moved out of the house and were either married or attending college. They exemplify a country western family with worn-out cowboy boots, old beat up trucks and a strong faith in God.

After getting permission from her family to enter the ICU, my wife and I crossed through the glass doors of Sarah's large room. I was taken back by all of the machines, monitors, tubes and personnel attending her. They were drawing blood samples and hanging up new bags of pain medication to slowly drip into her system, giving needed relief. Her hospital bed was elevated high in the air and I felt tiny as I slowly rolled into an unoccupied corner of the room. Her body was mostly paralyzed except for portions of one arm and hand. She had a feeding tube, severe blood pressure complications and a ventilator hose attached to her throat. Oh how I remembered that.

A daughter and son were sitting on the other side of the room — one on a phone call with the insurance company trying to get approvals, and the other with family members giving updates. A nurse was speaking with Sarah as her daughter hung up the phone and started walking toward us. I noticed Sarah was not communicating back to the nurse. I felt the pressure starting to build. What was I supposed to say? What am I expected to do here? Just because I'm paralyzed doesn't mean I have all the right answers. I began wondering if coming here was the right decision. Maybe I should have stayed home and made up some excuse why I couldn't do this. We spoke briefly to her daughter who tried introducing us to Sarah, just as her medicine was causing her to fall asleep. I'm not sure if she even saw me down here in my wheelchair or understood who we were.

As I watched her drift off to sleep, I remember what that was like. Being so uncomfortable you wanted to pull your hair out, but couldn't move to do it. Wondering if everything going on around you was just a dream. Fighting an unknown pain that won't stop, will suck the motivational drive right out of your soul. Being able to sleep, even for an hour, would at least temporarily give you a chance to regroup for the next round. We talked with both of her children for a while, learning more of Sarah's injuries and mental state. Her family told us they thought she was losing all hope. That worried me because without hope, you have nothing.

Later on as I pushed my wheelchair back to my truck, I looked over at Heather and said, "Wow, that was intense! She is in really bad shape and I'm not sure if she'll make it. That room was kind of scary to be in." She smiled as she put her hand on my shoulder and replied, "Honey. That's exactly what your room was like a few years ago."

The team you are assembling, whether you realize it or not, is sprinkled with individuals who will be the most supportive and loyal friends you've ever had.

Most of Sarah's family lived a few hours away from the hospital and it was very inconvenient to come visit and support her on a regular basis. We went back to see her at least twice a week and started bringing our children with us. Our family told her stories of great possibilities and gave her hope in all the progress she would make if she just kept fighting for what she wanted—what she needed. She loved seeing our children and they enjoyed sitting on her bed, holding her hand and laughing, just as they did for me.

Over the next few weeks, we worked with Sarah's family on what they needed to do to help her succeed. They started to renovate parts of their house and began looking for a wheelchair-accessible minivan. This would allow her to eventually live at home again with her family — what she wanted more than anything. Even if she couldn't walk, just being at home and trying to be a good wife and mother was enough.

Sarah was facing her fears and we saw extraordinary improvements mentally, and in her physical movement. She was beginning to believe it was possible. These were the best doctors, medicine and therapists in the area. Sarah was far from standing up and going for a jog, but she was beginning to eat on her own and was nearly free of the ventilator that assisted her breathing. Even with all of this incredible progress taking place, my wife and I started to see something happening that would soon alter this remarkable momentum.

One of Sarah's married daughters spent time at the hospital three to four times a week, even bringing her young children if she couldn't get a babysitter. Sarah's son who attended college showed up about twice a week, skipping a few classes if necessary. All the other children, though, were very sporadic and inconsistent in showing up at the hospital or even making phone calls. Her husband of many years found it difficult to visit, due to the necessity of managing the farm, earning money to pay the hospital bills and working on remodeling projects in the house for Sarah's possible return. What she really needed was him by her side and a consistent support system.

Sarah desperately wanted to protect and comfort her family like only a mother can, but the distance and less frequent visits made that tough. Each family member was battling their own method of coping, which included distancing themselves, arguing, avoiding, or denial. The son who was driving the car during the accident had only visited one time and barely spoke to his mother while he was there. I cannot fathom the guilt and regret he was battling as he viewed his mom lying in that hospital bed. I'm not sure anyone was willing to accept just how different the future was going to be for their family.

Her support system was beginning to dwindle and we couldn't fix it no matter how hard we tried.

Sarah began to get frustrated and disappointed as work on the house ran into problems and her family's calls and visits became more distant. Her length of stay in the hospital was longer than expected and she could sense something was wrong. Everything in her hopeful life seemed to suddenly freeze. The forward progression she was experiencing had stopped.

As her drive to survive began to weaken, so did her health. She caught pneumonia. This can be very dangerous for someone who is paralyzed because their lungs and diaphragm are compromised. It can be beat, though. She fought hard at first and felt a surge of energy when her two teenage children showed up to cheer her on, as did many friends. I even personally called her husband and asked if he would come see his wife and let her know she could count on him and she was needed. He said he would come visit as soon as he could.

Sarah was very worried that she wouldn't be able to fulfill her role as a mother and spouse again. There were still children at home she hadn't finished raising yet, and what about the grandchildren? She longed to be a part of all these experiences. Another worry was if her husband could handle running the family, work, and taking care of her at the same time.

Sarah's husband showed up shortly after my call without any of the children. We were so excited that this would be the boost she desired, to push her through the pneumonia and back on track. He was in her room for hours but still hadn't talked to her directly, only to others. The following day Sarah told us of the conversation between her and her husband, and what followed went so fast I couldn't believe what I was watching — what I was a part of.

Sarah's health dropped drastically the next day and she was put back in the ICU, the one she had worked so hard to get out of. The pneumonia that was almost gone returned in full force and she was put on a ventilator again to help her breathe. Against everyone's pleas, she chose not to do therapies anymore, causing her body to weaken and be even more susceptible to infection. Within just a few days from that pivotal night, she went unconscious and one day later, passed away. My young children were crying tears of sadness for someone they had grown to love when we told them she was gone. They wanted to go see her smiling face once more.

The night Sarah's husband left for the last time, there were tears rolling down her cheeks, disappearing into her hospital gown. They weren't tears of joy, but represented the hope leaving her body. Hope of her family and the way it once was. Hope of her being whole again. Hope of a future that she could accept and feel worth something.

During those few private minutes together her husband said that he loved her very much, but they were not able to finish remodeling the house for her to come home. With her health condition and physical limitations, it was going to be too hard and too expensive to have her live in their current residence. The family felt with the medical attention she would need it was in everyone's best interest if she lived in a nursing home and they would come visit. The closest facility able to care for her needs was almost two hours away from the family home. This was the knockout punch that sent her falling to the floor.

She spent most of her life loving, caring, teaching, sacrificing and serving this family. They were her life. No more big Sunday dinners, late nights worrying for a teenager to get home, or holding hands with her husband on the couch after a long day.

Sarah felt as if her support system had collapsed. During the five days her health was quickly declining, we prayed that somehow Sarah could find the desire to fight and hold out for hope. Without her core support group, she wasn't strong enough to continue on. Sarah lost her will to live. She needed to feel the reinforcement and reassurance of a strong support system to succeed. Don't we all?

Here are five qualities your support system must collectively possess:

1. You can always trust them.
2. They love you enough to tell you what you need to hear at times, not just what you want to hear.
3. Achieving your potential is a top priority to them.
4. They will not try to control you, but be patient, encourage, and work with you.
5. They're a good listener who tries to understand your needs.

It can be an arduous task to get from our current situation to where we want to be, without the assistance of others. Of course there are individuals who have done it, but their stories are far less common. Through sharing our goals, fears, successes and failures with those we trust, we magnify our opportunities for personal success many times over. They get to know you, the real you, and then start to invest their own personal time and talents into your progression. The team you are assembling, whether you realize it or not, is sprinkled with individuals who will be the most supportive and loyal friends you've ever had.

NathanOgden.com

CHAPTER QUESTIONS:

What support system do I have in my life right now? (This may include family, friends, medical, a faith-based community, support group, 12-step group, club or activity.)

_____

_____

_____

_____

What strengths do those individuals exhibit?

_____

_____

_____

_____

Are there some who mean well but are more of a hindrance than help? Can I distance that relationship so I'm only surrounded by positive influences?

_____

_____

_____

_____

_____

What specific steps will I take to expand my support network? What will I do this week?

_____

_____

_____

_____

_____

_____

_____

_____

9

~~~~~~~~~~~~~~~~~~~~~~~~

Don't Fight The Flood

*"It's amazing, how far you can go;
just because someone believed in you!"*
—GBATISTE

I POSSES A STRONG BELIEF in surrounding yourself with loyal family and friends when going through a challenging time or while pushing yourself to accomplish lofty goals. However, I have learned that some of the people who have cared the most about my success and well-being, are those I didn't always give credit to — my doctor, nurse, Sunday school teacher, therapist, coach, boss, scout leader, distant neighbor, coworkers, professors, classmates, and even those I've never even met, but believed in me.

The beautiful thing about someone being loyal to you is there's a tremendous amount of trust built, making you want to be loyal to them. Over time this can turn into an amazing relationship that is indestructible. The following experience solidified in my mind what a superior support system looks like.

Before my neck breaks, I had always been very competitive and active in many sports and the outdoors. I gave it everything I had to win the game and enjoyed my share of success. It used to really irritate my in-laws because everything became a competition, even if it was playing cards or shoveling snow. I loved pushing my body's limits and the energy and excitement when a game came down to the final few seconds. This thrilling sensation can become an addiction.

After being paralyzed — twice — I still wanted to be active, but everything I tried was much harder and didn't seem as fun as before. I used to create excuses to rationalize why I wasn't chasing after these activities as much anymore. Remember the chapter on excuses and my trump card? The first excuse is very simple — I mean come on, I am a quadriplegic who is supposed to ride around in an electric wheelchair and have people take care of me. Right?

The true test of someone who genuinely wants you to succeed is they will never quit trying.

The other is that we weren't sure if I could do anything too strenuous because of my physical limitations. Due to my paralysis I am unable to sweat throughout most of my body, causing my core temperature to rise extremely fast. This also means it takes a long time to cool myself down. Another complication is my weak diaphragm and lung function suppresses my ability to breathe deeply enough to provide my muscles the oxygen they need to perform at a higher level. If I don't watch these closely, I can experience heat stroke, painful spasms, blurred vision, severe vomiting, or even death. Deep down inside, though, I still had a burning desire to push myself once again.

My wife (captain of my support system) did some research on her own because she wanted to see me do something athletic again. Even if it meant just going on a family bike ride around the neighborhood. With a little convincing, we had a hand bike specifically built for me that I could power with my arms. When it arrived I was excited but very skeptical as everything else had been a letdown so far. The bike looked like a really cool adult-sized tricycle that was lower to the ground. The handlebars also doubled as the pedals allowing me to steer and generate power simultaneously.

Our neighbor, Steve, and my wife, Heather, lifted me down into the bike seat, strapped my hands onto the pedals and cinched a tie down around the seat back and my chest, to keep me from falling out on either side. They pulled the strap so tight I remember it being hard to breathe. It felt exhilarating to ride again and have control over my speed and direction. I didn't make it very far that first ride and it hurt quite a bit, but it put a smile on my face and the faces of my family riding next to me. As exciting as it was, I'll bet I only rode the bike three more times that summer and then it sat in our garage, untouched. I told myself, "I can't do it. It's too hard. My arms are not strong enough, and I will never compete again." Not only did I use these excuses on my family, but worst of all I used them on myself. And I believed it; I really started to believe it.

The true test of someone who genuinely wants you to succeed is they will never quit trying. That next spring my wife and a good friend John Ashby, came across an opportunity for me to compete in a half triathlon. John had completed full triathlons before and was very knowledgeable about what it might take for me. They sat me down and began explaining this idea and what I would need to do to accomplish the sprint version of a half triathlon. I would need to swim in cold lake water for 1.25 miles, ride my bike 12 miles and run the last 3 miles. Obviously the running portion was going to be a problem so we decided to bike the last 3 miles making it a total of 15 miles pedaling with my limited arm strength.

As they continued to make their pitch, I began forming the excuses in my mind as to why I couldn't do this. I took a deep breath, looked them in the eyes, and blurted out, "Okay, I'll do it!" I couldn't let this idea of what I thought a quadriplegic should be control my life. With only a couple months to train and those I trusted willing to help me, we went to work.

It was a hot August race day and I was a little nervous. I wondered how I would do, if my kids would be proud, how would my body react, would this be as fun as I want it to be, and could I actually survive. My wife was genuinely concerned for my health, always making sure there was an ambulance nearby. The temperature could reach 98° by noon triggering life-threatening complications.

It was go time, so four people squeezed me into a wetsuit and dropped me into the cold water to start the race. I began swimming with all the energy and adrenalin I possessed, determined not to come in first but definitely not place last. I'm pretty sure I demonstrated the best backstroke in the entire field of contestants that day. It was exhilarating to be competing again, something I thought I left on the X-ray table years before. I was in last place but quickly gaining on … no one. My youngest brother Devin swam beside me the whole time to encourage me and make sure I didn't lose my direction and swim the wrong way.

After the swimming portion, my wetsuit was ripped off and I was carried by Devin and my brother-in-law, Nathan, up to my bike for the second leg of the race — using the exact same muscles that were worn out from swimming. I was all strapped in tight and began biking up a steep parking lot just to get to the main road. Hundreds of spectators watched and cheered as I slowly went by. I think they were more excited that they could now leave the park than they were about what I was accomplishing, but in my mind we'll just say it was for me.

The outside temperature rose quickly into the 90s and we had to make frequent stops so Devin could dump ice water over my entire body to keep me from overheating. With my family watching and yelling I felt an immense strength and support while still in last place and falling farther behind. I was getting so far behind that as I passed a road barrier placed to protect the competitors, I noticed the police officers taking it down so traffic could resume as usual. This was a mental blow and I started contemplating if it was worth it. Then I saw my kids hanging out the windows of our truck clapping enthusiastically for their dad as I peddled by. I can go another mile, I thought. They need to see me go another mile.

About mile 9 into the biking portion I felt my body screaming at me to STOP! My muscles began to tighten and shake, each breath was getting harder to grasp, my nerve pain was accelerating, and my vision was significantly blurred. My core body temperature was getting too high and I couldn't cool down. I felt sick and wanted to quit. I'm pushing my body to limits that it should not be pushed! My life could be in jeopardy if I keep going!

As much as I wanted to stop I knew I could make it three more miles to the next transition point and end there. I asked my brother to ride his bike in front of me so I had someone to follow since my vision wasn't clear. "Just a little further, keep on pedaling, Nathan, I can do this," I said to myself.

I slowly rolled into the town park and stopped at the last transition point of the race. This is where you drop off your bike and start running the final leg. It was stationed right next to the finish line. As my support team began giving me Gatorade, dumping water on my head, and squeezing energy gels into my mouth, I could see the finish line ahead of me off to the left. I can just pedal a little farther and then turn straight through to the finish line. I was so weak at this point that if I weren't strapped onto my bike I would have collapsed into the hard pavement. I was hot, exhausted and physically and mentally depleted. There wasn't anything left for me to give. I had gone far enough, no one would think any less of me if I stopped right here.

I began making excuses. I'm a quadriplegic—everyone will think I'm a hero just for making it this far. Unable to fully open my eyes I could hear the comments around me. "We're so proud of you. You have come so far. What a great example. You don't need to go any farther, you have gone far enough." I warily looked up at the finish line and then at my wife and children. I have to finish the race, I must move forward. I refuse to let the "q" in quadriplegic stand for quit. I am more powerful than that!

Without saying a word, I took off pedaling the last three miles as fast as my feeble arms would allow. There were only 30 minutes left in the race and then they shut it down. Somehow I've got to come in faster than that, though it didn't look possible. All by myself pedaling on a skinny sidewalk, I began to think that even though I wouldn't finish in time, this whole adventure was still worth it. After the first mile, I could hear footsteps coming up from behind me on the left. It's probably my brother. As my arms kept going round and round I looked over to see my 11-year-old son jogging beside me.

It's not how many individuals you have on your side, but the stability of their character and purpose.

"What are you doing, Kyler? You didn't train for this. It's a long way to run. Maybe you should head back." He then said something I will never forget. "I want to run with you dad. You don't have to be alone. We can do this together." I had to turn my head so he wouldn't see the tears in my eyes. We all know dads don't cry while doing hard manly sports in front of their kids. Right? I could be wrong about that.

This gave me the energy and drive to push harder and dig deeper. What a selfless act of courage and love put on display by an 11-year-old boy. Or should I say young man. We talked and ran together until I noticed three other images come into view. During the last half mile my three daughters ages 5, 7 and 13 caught up to us and all the athletes and spectators cheered as we crossed the finish line together. I couldn't be more impressed with them and proud of what we accomplished together as I finished the race three minutes before it closed. I accomplished my goal, earned a medal, and received the trophy of a chicken for coming in last. I'm okay with that. No one else got a trophy.

About to cross the finish line with my children

Completing a half triathlon would not have been possible if I were left to do it alone. I needed a team of loyal supporters who would not give up on me even when I wanted to give up on myself. They pushed me, motivated me, loved me and stayed by my side when it felt impossible to succeed. John didn't just give his expert advice on how to compete in the half triathlon, but he even put on his ugly tight biking shorts and swimsuit and physically lifted, pulled, and carried me along.

People like that are your superior support system. It's not how many individuals you have on your side, but the stability of their character and purpose. Their purpose is to see you succeed. When you don't have the strength to take another step, they are there to lift you up and nudge your foot forward again — always.

There will be times through this process when you experience loneliness, betrayal and darkness all around. You may feel similar to Sarah who was drowning in despair. These are the moments you must listen for the soft footsteps of someone who cares running up beside you. It may not be who you expect, but will always be who you need. As much as we want to leave all the tough decisions for others to decide, it still always comes down to one person's choice. Yours! You must chose to help yourself before anyone can truly help you.

You must chose to help yourself before anyone can truly help you.

The ticket to having a superior support system is to be a valuable contributor in that system. The more you focus on building up those around you, the larger your capacity to serve becomes. This creates a tight-knit attachment to each other that's nearly impossible to break.

The following is a list of my support team for this awesome accomplishment:

- ❖ Steve Russo: Assembled my bike and helped me on my first ride.
- ❖ Race manager: Altered the rules a bit so I qualified to compete.
- ❖ Ken's Bicycle Warehouse/Access Van's: Sponsored me to compete in race.
- ❖ Dr. Dubose: Followed and monitored health.
- ❖ Athletes and spectators: Constantly cheered me on, giving me hope.
- ❖ Friends and extended family: Encouraged me to cross the finish-line.
- ❖ John Ashby (friend): Helped Heather convince me to race and then trained with me for both biking and swimming. His efforts were monumental to my success.
- ❖ Devin Ogden (brother): Swam by my side and rode his bike near me the whole way. He should have received a medal for completing the race. He was selfless!
- ❖ Jolene Ogden (mom): Took pictures and gave support throughout the race.
- ❖ My children (Seniya, Kyler, Malani, Cortlyn): Trained with me and cheered me on through all the ups and downs. Never gave up on me.

- ❖ Heather Ogden (wife): My biggest cheerleader, motivator, instigator and undoubting believer I could ever have. She has more faith and hope in my abilities than I do. Everything I achieve is made possible because of her loving touch.

CHAPTER QUESTIONS:

Who are my top three supporters.

_____

_____

_____

_____

_____

_____

Why do they support me?

_____

_____

_____

_____

_____

Whose list am I on and why have they chosen me?

_____

_____

_____

_____

_____

_____

Who should I be helping right now but I'm not? Why not? What will I do to change that?

_____

_____

_____

_____

_____

When is the last time I thanked them for being there?

_____

_____

_____

10

It's Time To Swim

AFTER A LONG TIRING HIKE I REACH THE TOP of a steep rocky ridge and the view is breathtaking. Just a quarter-mile further down the seldom-used trail lies the beautiful clear water of Hook Ear Lake, nestled beneath the tall mountain peaks. I can't wait to catch a big rainbow trout swimming beneath its surface. Tightening the laces on my boots, I walk briskly down the trail when... Beep! Beep! Beep! As my alarm goes off I'm instantaneously transported from high in the Rocky Mountains to my dark hotel room in Salt Lake City, Utah. Even though I'm paralyzed, it doesn't mean I can't still dream of walking.

A few minutes later there's a knock, and the door slowly opens as I hear a voice say, "Mr. Ogden, is it okay if I come in?" Over the next hour and a half, a caregiver helps me in the bathroom, transferring me in and out of the shower, and helping me get dressed for the day.

I'm then lifted by another stranger into the front seat of a van, pulling out my dress shirt someone else just finished tucking in.

On our way to the conference center, we casually talk about the weather and then the driver awkwardly asks how I was injured. Two hours after arriving at our destination, a couple more men lift my wheelchair up onto a big stage with me still sitting in it. The lapel mic is turned on as the lights in the room begin to focus on me. It's time! Time to lead by example!

For years I have spoken to many audiences of all different sizes, but now it is my career. I always knew speaking was what I was meant to do since the neck breaks, and where I would feel the most satisfied — and happy. This career is where I can make the biggest difference in telling my story of living unfrozen. But I created excuses, justified my lack of progression and told myself it wasn't worth the effort to speak professionally because no one would pay to hear me — no one would listen to what I had to say anyway. The negativity I told myself froze my potential in its tracks.

You can't leave the batteries out of your flashlight and expect it to give light when you need it. Thanks to the messages I have shared in my book, the fear has melted away and the possibilities are right in front of me. Because I found the strength to break through what I thought were my limits, I'm now honored to hear stories of others who have been inspired by my efforts. I'm forever thankful to those who inspire me. A slowly thawing block of ice will eventually break free, plunging into a pool of water below causing a magnificent ripple effect that is beautiful to behold. Will you be the start of a ripple that affects thousands?

The most important lesson I have learned since that snowy ski hill 14 years ago is to "keep moving forward!" My testimony of this principle is rock solid and will never change. As long as you are progressing, no matter how fast or slow, it becomes nearly impossible to lose all hope; hope that your life will get better, hope that you will make it through this trial, hope that your goals and dreams will come true.

In the summer of 2015, my wife and I sold our house in Idaho and moved our family of six to Virginia. Why? Because we needed to shake up our lives a bit. We needed to leave our family and friends and allow ourselves to travel far outside our comfort zone for a while. Both of us felt inspired that this is what we needed to do and where we needed to go. If it wasn't for this move across the country, there is no way I would have finished this book in just seven months. This situation has provided new opportunities not prevalent before. Growing up it never even crossed my mind that I could write a book that people would read. Thanks to moving to Virginia, I have now *become* an author. Our family will never regret this adventure and our experiences on the East Coast.

As we allow our greatest desires to melt away what keeps us frozen, the water begins to flow. Water always adapts to the form it's placed in. Whether a small cup, a large vase or a vast reservoir, it fills that shape instantly. Our Father in Heaven often places us in forms we don't like and are not comfortable in. Those who possess this water-like attribute, the ability to adapt and fill this role, will find their purpose and have the greatest chance for happiness and success. Thus those who fight their situation and are angry about the mold they're placed in, struggle to find peace. It's not a coincidence that those who are most formless, like water, are also the ones that shape our world the most.

The new goals and adventures I have planned for the future will be more exciting and fulfilling than anything I've done in the past. If you do hard things, you will enjoy extraordinary rewards. Following these superior systems has allowed me to *move* from paralysis to progress.

You are strong, you are powerful, you are capable, and most importantly, you are worth it! Keep attacking your doubts and fears, ignore the negative comments and thoughts constantly being put in your head, and continually strive to lift those around you. As you seize each moment with confidence, you will *become* the person you've always desired to be and live a life *Unfrozen.*

PHOTOS OF OUR
OGDEN ADVENTURES

Oregon Coast – Daddy daughter time on the beach

Kyler and me at the fair

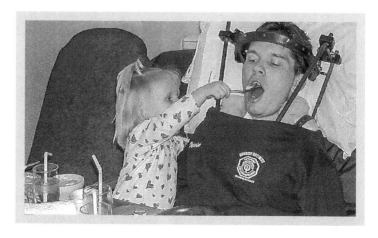

Seniya giving me strength in more ways than one

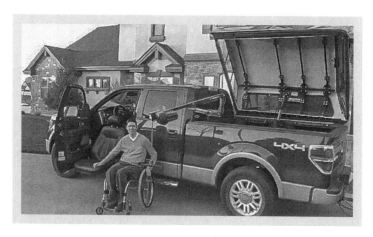

My (Transformer) truck

Our family motto

Snow skiing at Park City, Utah

Malani pushing me at Disneyland

Skydiving tandem — strategic landing required

Family picture in McCall, Idaho

Swimming with my brother Devin to start the Half
Triathlon

Riding my hand-powered bike during the race

Motivating a gym filled with students

Visiting Outer Banks, NC while living in Virginia

About The Author

NATHAN OGDEN has spent years motivating and inspiring audiences on how to conquer their fears and *move* from paralysis to progress. He uses his unique life-changing experiences in controlling choices when faced with adversity, to train a vast variety of groups from elementary schools to executives throughout the country. With his engaging and energetic personality, Nathan connects with his audiences immediately and delivers invaluable principles they can relate to and act upon.

Nathan's drive is evident in how he lives his life as a quadriplegic, by not allowing paralysis to determine his aspirations. Since breaking his neck, he has experienced river rafting, snow skiing, water skiing, snorkeling, skydiving, *completing* a half triathlon and repelling into a slot canyon near Zion's National Park. Nathan's courage and determination gives hope and power to all who know him and hear his message.

Nathan's true joy is found spending time with his wife Heather, and raising their four children in Idaho. He is passionate about finding new adventures to experience with his family, and helping others realize their potential.

He holds a BA in business management with an emphasis in human resources from Boise State University.

Connect with Nathan:

Email: ogdennathan@hotmail.com
Website: www.NathanOgden.com
Facebook: www.facebook.com/nathan.ogden.39
Twitter: @NathanDOgden

Book Nathan as a keynote speaker
and trainer at *www.NathanOgden.com*

94834271R00098

Made in the USA
Columbia, SC
05 May 2018